John Patrick's Casino Poker

John Patrick's Casino Poker

A Professional Gambler's Guide to Winning

John Patrick

A LYLE STUART BOOK
Published by Carol Publishing Group

A Lyle Stuart Book
Published by Carol Publishing Group
Lyle Stuart is a registered trademark of Carol Communications, Inc.

For editorial, sales and distribution, and questions regarding rights and
permissions, write to Carol Publishing Group, 120 Enterprise Avenue, Secaucus,
NJ 07094

In Canada: Canadian Manda Group, One Atlantic Avenue, Suite 105, Toronto,
Ontario M6K 3E7

Carol Publishing Group Books are available at special discounts for bulk
purchases, for sales promotions, fund-raising, or educational purposes.

Special editions can be created to specifications.

Manufactured in the United States of America
12 11 10 9 8 7 6 5 4 3 2 1

Library of Congress Cataloging-in-Publication Data

Patrick, John, 1932–
    John Patrick's casino poker : a professional gambler's guide to
winning / John Patrick.
    p.   cm.
    "A Lyle Stuart book."
    ISBN 0-8184-0592-9 (pbk.)
    1. Poker.   2. Gambling.   I. Title.
GV1251.P28 1996
795.41'2—dc20   96-34879
                                             CIP

Dedication

This is my tenth book covering a phase of gambling.
And all of them were dedicated to my family. No reason to
change now because they are everything that counts in my life.
To my Mom and Dad and my daughters, Lori and Colleen

Thank you again!

Contents

PART I: POKER

1   Poker: The Beginning   3
2   Intimidation: Casino Poker   5
3   The Author and Poker   7
4   Terms   9
5   The Big Four   11
6   The Little Three   13
7   Seven-Card Stud   15
8   Tells   17
9   Reading the Players   20
10 Why Do You Play Poker?   23
11 Reading the Cards   25
12 Percentages in Poker   27
13 Wrapping Up the Introduction   30

PART II: BANKROLL

14 Bankroll: The Start   33
15 Sessions   35
16 Loss Limits   37
17 Win Goals   39
18 Short Bankroll   41
19 Scared Bankroll   43
20 Wrapping Up Bankroll   45

PART III: STUD

21 Seven-Card Stud   47
22 Casino: Seven-Card Stud Basic Rules   50
23 Casino: Stud   53

24	Third Street	56
25	Variables: Third Street	59
26	Wrapping Up Third Street	61
27	Session Money	63
28	Fourth Street	65
29	Fourth Street Fallacies	67
30	Wrapping Up Fourth Street	69
31	Fifth Street	71
32	Fifth Street Analogies	73
33	Wrapping Up Fifth Street	75
34	Stud: Sixth Street	77
35	Sixth Street Varieties	80
36	Wrapping Up Sixth Street	82
37	Seventh Street	84
38	Wrapping Up Seventh Street	86
39	Flushes and Straights	88
40	Synopsis of Stud	90

PART IV: HI/LO

41	Hi/Lo Stud	93
42	House Rules in Casino Style	96
43	Keying the Game	98
44	Third Street	100
45	Fourth Street	102
46	Reading Players	104
47	Wrapping Up Fourth Street	106
48	Fifth Street	108
49	Wrapping Up Fifth Street	110
50	Sixth Street	112
51	Wrapping Up Sixth Street	114
52	Seventh Street	116
53	Raising	118
54	Bluffing	120
55	Wrapping Up Seventh Street	122
56	Community Card	124
57	Wrapping It Up	126

PART V: TEXAS HOLD 'EM

58 Texas Hold 'Em 127
59 The Game 129
60 Beginning 131
61 Rankings 133
62 Terms 135
63 Quick Review 137
64 Reading the Cards 139
65 Reading the Flop 141
66 Practice 143
67 Positive Betting 145
68 Turn Card 147
69 Theories 149
70 Raising Intelligently 151
71 The River 153
72 Power of Observation 155
73 Reality 157

PART VI: MONEY MANAGEMENT

74 Hold 'Em: Money Management 159
75 Hold 'Em: Need 161
76 Hold 'Em: Playing Tight 163
77 Do You Want Money Management? 165
78 Poker: Betting Moves 167
79 Poker: Odds 169
80 Hold 'Em: Playing Loose or Tight? 171
81 Hold 'Em: Betting Patterns 173
82 Drawing to Dead Hands 175
83 Money Management: Is It Important? 177
84 Winding Down Money Management 179
85 Wrapping Up Money Management 181

PART VII: DISCIPLINE

86 Discipline 183
87 Win Goal 184
88 Guarantee and Excess 185
89 Handling the Excess 187

90	Can You Do It?	189
91	Loss Limits Again	190
92	Accepting Small Returns	191
93	Reality	193
94	The Professional Poker Player	195
95	The Author and Discipline	197
96	Reality II	199
97	Wrapping UP Poker Knowledge	202
98	Wrapping Up Discipline	205
99	The Ultimate Goal	206

John Patrick's Casino Poker

Poker

1

Poker: The Beginning

Read this chapter! I want you to refer back to this chapter 3,623 times during your trip through this book. Not because there is a lot of poker-playing information in it, but because it encompasses what is covered on the following pages.

First, I assume you know how to play poker, so I will address you as a player who knows the object of the game but wants to improve to the next level. *These messages are aimed strictly at the intermediate player and not the advanced student.* Therein lies the message I want you to absorb. I intend to take the novice, the new player, the cautious player, the neophyte to the next level.

I will concentrate on playing in casinos because they are becoming more and more popular each day. People who have been playing weekly house games are now looking to enter the casino to try their luck, but are like fish out of water.

This book explains how to conduct yourself at low- to medium-skill casino tables. A few chapters also are dedicated to house games. We will stick strictly to seven-card stud, seven-card stud hi/lo, and Texas Hold 'Em. To try and cram in Pineapple, Omaha, five-card draw, and the tremendous array of other games would take away from the real purpose of the book.

Since seven-card stud is the most popular game, we'll go in that direction. If you want other casino games and sports handicapping, you can refer to my nine previous books covering games such as craps, roulette, blackjack, baccarat, slots, and football betting.

Poker is by far the most difficult to explain because of the various combinations that arise during the course of play. There are thousands of situations that come up on third street and fourth street, with another thousand variables based on your opponents' hands and especially the makeup of the different combinations. Bottom line is I could set up hundreds of examples and still not put a dent in the total number of variables. There are just too many to illustrate, and I'd end up leaving out some that will come up the next time you play. There are lots of books on the market that offer loads of examples, and after trying to concentrate on the first eighty-three, I lose interest and just end up reading numbers.

So while I'll give you some examples, they will be limited. I'm more concerned with you learning the REAL way to gain an edge in poker.

This book is designed to zero in on how to take advantage of weak opponents, how to cut losses, when to leave a game, when to increase your bets, when to pull back, and how to accept small consistent wins.

A fair group of people who have written books on how to win at poker will vehemently disagree with my theories. I don't give a rat's tail if you like them or not, but I know they work. You bought the book to get an insight into winning at poker, so why not give these ideas a decent shot?

To repeat: I am focusing only on seven-card stud, seven-card stud hi/lo, and Texas Hold 'Em as played in the casinos and for the intermediate player only. If you consider yourself an advanced player, you'll have to await my advanced book, but at least you can check out the direction I'm going.

2

Intimidation: Casino Poker

Don't scoff at the word *intimidation*—it applies to most of us in life, and we are all faced with situations which make us think twice about pulling the trigger. A lot of you may be good poker players but get a little queasy about the prospect of playing in a casino with a table of strangers. In fact, there are many people who have approached me outside a poker room and admitted to being skeptical about walking inside. I show them how easy it is, walk them through the exercise, and in some cases continue through the act of "buying in" and staying for a few hands.

Yeah, I know a lot of you heroes were born with brass brains, so it doesn't bother you. I am talking to you few people who are intimidated in casinos and can't get up the moxie to enter that poker room. There is nothing, I mean absolutely, positively nothing, to get bent out of shape about. All the players at that table are regular people with the same purpose as you—to win a few bucks at a game they're good at.

Let's briefly walk through a buy-in. You're in front of the poker room. Go to the front desk, tell them which game you'd like to play, and give them your name or initials. The games are:

$1–$3 seven-card stud
$3–$6 seven-card stud
$2–$4 hi/lo
$2–$4 Texas Hold 'Em
$5–$10 seven-card stud

If there is an opening at your choice, you'll be seated. If not, they will page you. If, for example, you are seated at a table playing $3–$6 seven-card stud, the game will proceed as follows:

1. The house dealer announces the rules, ante, table limits, checking procedures, etc.
2. Take out $100 (example) and place it in front of you.
3. The dealer gives you chips after completion of the current hand.
4. If it is an ante game (example, 25¢), just toss your quarter into the pot. If you need change, DO NOT make it yourself. The dealer is the only one who can make change.
5. You'll be dealt three cards, two down and one up.
6. Low card MUST bet.
7. If you call or raise, just toss the chips in front of you. The dealer will use the rake to pull them into the pot.
8. If you fold, toss cards face down to the dealer.
9. The dealer calls the game and after the first three cards, betting reverts to high-hand first.
10. If you raise, it must be in one continuous move with no delay.
11. If you wish to stay in the hand but are out of chips, merely state, "all in." You are still in the game for the amount of the pot you called. All subsequent betting will be in a separate pot for the remaining players.
12. At the end of the game, dealer announces the winner and pushes the pot to the winner.

The house keeps approximately 5 percent as the game progresses, with a set maximum per hand. Any player has the right to see the hand of another player when the hand is completed, even if the asker has dropped out.

There you have a simple explanation of a situation that surely should not be intimidating. Each of these points will be dealt with in time. Just understand there is no reason to be scared.

3

The Author and Poker

I love to play poker, and naturally I am good at it, otherwise I wouldn't play. But don't get the idea I win every session, let alone every hand. That's impossible. Give the other players credit—they are also good players. They are your mortal enemies during the course of that session. They are looking for weaknesses in your play, just as you are searching for their Waterloo.

Growing up in New Jersey, I became aware of playing cards through my best friend, my dad, who was a fabulous pinochle player and excelled at poker, canasta, and gin rummy because he remembered every single card dealt. (This was long before card counting became an issue.) In those days families engaged in card games because TV was in its infancy and family life was much, much different than it is today—but that's another story.

My dad always beat me at these games but at the same time he was teaching me to be better. I listened and learned because I wanted to make money when "the guys" set up penny and 5¢ games on the weekends. My father was NOT a gambler, but he knew cards and how to pick the horses. He did not like gambling, but his son sure did and learned from the best.

As the years passed, I grew into playing poker in the local bowling alley after hours, then the weekly, biweekly, and nightly games. When Bret and Bart Maverick arrived on the TV scene, I was hooked beyond any chance of returning to my grammar-school goal of being a priest.

When I got to Vegas I was young, dumb, and ambitious. The

7

dumb part was exploited most. I thought being a "great player" from New Jersey gave me a leg up on beating all those "hicks" in Las Vegas. Man, did they bring me down to earth and give me my first taste of reality.

In those days Vegas was just coming into its own. The players were experienced, no-holds-barred, sharp, calculating, merciless assassins who jumped all over every greenhorn who thought he belonged in their league. To say they taught me what the real world of poker was all about is like saying I think Loni Anderson has a cute figure. Understatement. They hit me high, low, sideways, upside down, and inside out. It was an expensive experience, but you either learned to play right or you took up clipping magazine coupons to save a buck.

But even great poker players can't guarantee getting good hands. The important thing is how you play the hands you are dealt. I'll refer to this over and over again. Poker is the ability to play the hands you're dealt against other barracudas who also know how to use every weapon at their disposal.

I will bore you with this statement until you realize how important it is: A good poker player knows how to get the most out of a good hand and when to cut losses with a bad hand. A bad poker player doesn't know how to take advantage of good hands or when to cut losses with bad ones.

This message is more important than giving you an untold number of examples because situations change depending on the different players involved. I am a good player, but if I don't get the cards, how the deuce can I expect to beat other players? I can't, so I run. There will be another hand. It took me a long time to absorb this message, but it finally sunk in.

Don't wait as long as I did!

4

Terms

Let's touch on a few terms you may not be familiar with, just so we can keep the messages flowing. I won't go over the obvious ones as I assume you have reached the stage of intermediate play. If you think tip has to do with the end of an asparagus spear, you're in a little trouble. And if you think ante means that lady who pulls the strings on your favorite uncle, you're obviously in the wrong book and at the wrong game.

RAKE: The house take per game.

BUY-IN: The amount of money you enter a game with. Rules usually require ten times the amount of the lowest game stakes. Example: In a $5–$10 game, buy-in must be $50.

FORCED BET: The low card MUST bet by suit (clubs, diamonds, hearts, spades).

BLIND: In Hold 'Em, the two seats to the left of the designated dealer MUST bet the amounts set by game limits.

BUTTON: In Hold 'Em, the object moved around the table by the house dealer to designate who bets first for that hand.

BURN CARD: The house dealer "burns" or "buries" the first card face down before every succeeding round of cards.

MUCK: The pile of unused cards and discarded dead hands.

CARDS SHOW: When the dealer determines the winning hand, based on cards showing. If he makes a mistake, the other players can point it out.

COMMUNITY CARD: If the dealer sees there are not enough cards to finish the round, he will bury a card and declare the next card "community," which is used by all remaining players.

FLOP: In Texas Hold 'Em, flop is the three-card turnover after cards are dealt and players bet on their first two cards.

POT LIMIT: The maximum bet allowed any time during the game is the size of the pot at any given moment.

TABLE STAKES: No players can bet or raise more than the total amount of the chips he has on the table.

ALL IN: A player can make or call a bet down to his last chip, but he is only involved in the pot up to that point. Subsequent bets by other players are kept in a separate pot.

SIDE POT: The separate pot started for players who continue betting after a player calls all in. That player is not involved in any subsequent side pots.

There are eight million stories in the naked city and there are eighty million terms used in poker games. Most are cute or self-explanatory and would only serve to use up space in lieu of more important items. I listed a handful just to clarify situations I'll use in this book. Upcoming chapters will go deeper into some of these terms in relation to how they affect which game you should get involved in based on your knowledge of that game, bankroll, and skill.

I could have inserted pictures of cards denoting ace of diamonds or four of clubs or jack of spades and made you think I was a real slicker. Instead I decided to save space and explain which cards are used in certain examples. For instance, instead of showing the three cards mentioned above, I will simply refer to them as AD, 4C, and JS.

You should get the point. If you don't, you probably think a check is that piece of paper you forget to send to your ex-wife each month.

5

The Big Four

No matter which type game you play, there are four things you'd better bring to the battle. These won't guarantee you a winner every session, but without all these items you don't have a prayer of competing.

I call them the Big Four. You'd best memorize them:

Bankroll
Knowledge of the Game
Money Management
Discipline

You've probably heard them before and maybe some of you even understand what they are. But if you are lacking even one of these ingredients, you're in for a rough time. Even in poker, which relies on other intangibles to allow you to be successful, it all reverts back to the Big Four.

BANKROLL

In the casinos, when you play craps, blackjack, or whatever your choice, the amount of money you lay out is always significant because of table minimums and mandatory action bets. In poker, you can play in a no-ante game, get three cards to review for nothing, and last a long time on a handful of chips. But playing with a short or "scared" bankroll will eventually take its toll.

KNOWLEDGE OF THE GAME

Just knowing the game of poker and its objective ain't gonna help you determine when a guy is bluffing or ante-stealing or false-raising throughout a poker session. Knowledge of poker includes the ability to know the little moves made by each of the players in that game. From there, you take that knowledge and jam it down the throat of your opponent. You look for flaws in the other players' games and wait for the time to use your knowledge to either grab a pot or cut your losses.

MONEY MANAGEMENT

In poker, money management is even more important than it is in casino table games. That's because there are betting situations and variations popping up and down every time a card hits the table. How much to bet, when to check, when to raise, when to drop, when to check and raise, and when to call, come up every time you get a card and a new sequence of betting starts. Herein is the key to becoming a successful poker player. It's called money management.

DISCIPLINE

This never changes. The ability or brains or guts to know when to quit is the mark of a successful gambler. The lack thereof is the demise of most players. A good poker player can last a long time with a short bankroll, but he needs the discipline to know when to pack it in. Yet most players refuse to acquire the discipline it takes to become successful.

How many of you have the guts to follow these rules?

I will focus on each aspect of the Big Four in a separate section. I wonder if you'll see yourself in the areas that point out the dumb things we all do at a poker table.

6

The Little Three

Theory! Logic! Trends! Although not as powerful as the Big Four, the Little Three are important if for no other reason than to cut losses. The biggest trap poor poker players fall into is their refusal to learn the smart moves it takes to raise their game to the next level.

We grew up learning how to play penny ante seven-card stud and five-card draw from our parents. As soon as we became aware of the rules, we'd grab a handful of pennies and join the family game. It was fun, challenging, and sometimes rewarding. We pictured ourselves as good poker players. Well, if you bring that limited amount of knowledge into a $1–$3 game in the casino, you'll understand the phrase "A fool and his money are soon parted."

The vultures at these tables make real vultures seem like doves. They can spot a weakness, suck you in, and drain you dry. You won't know what hit you.

That's why we have the Little Three:

Theory
Logic
Trends

THEORY

Theory is opinion. Everyone has an opinion on everything, and that's as it should be. It doesn't matter if you agree or disagree with a person's theory. Who's to say who is right or wrong? I have an opinion, or theory, on how to gamble—in this case, how to play poker. You can agree or disagree with this theory. It is very, very conservative, but I believe that is the proper way to attack this game. You might have a different theory. Then go write a book. This is my book and my theory.

LOGIC

Logic is approaching every situation from a controlled, so-called intelligent standpoint. Anything to do with gambling should be approached in this way because there has to be a reason for each decision. Setting your opponent up for a bluff might be construed as reverse logic, but from the standpoint of the "setter-upper," it is a logical move. You'll see what I mean as we go along.

TRENDS

Here is the biggie in the Little Three. In fact, someday I may move it a step higher and form the Big Five. Trends dominate in gambling whether they are hot trends or cold trends, and taking advantage of them is important. If you are not aware that trends are out there, you can't hope to know how to use them when they're going your way or how to avoid them when they're working against you! This is a biggie and should be so noted. Trends dominate. Or have I said that before?

Now you have a list of the seven things you must have in order to compete. But will you learn how to put the knowledge to work? I'm not sure because it ain't easy to be a disciplined player.

The reward is money, but there are dorks that don't realize it.

7

Seven-Card Stud

Poker and all its variations is by far the most popular card game in the country. It encompasses betting, bluffing, setups, reading your opponent, remembering cards, checking and raising, and potential big payoffs. Every time a new game comes on the scene, it offers bigger challenges, offshoots, and variables, but it still comes back to the basic premise of poker—especially seven-card stud. That's why this book will concentrate on that game and zero in on the lower-limit games that are available at the casinos—$1–$3, $3–$6, and $5–$10 seven-card stud.

Maybe you've gotten your feet wet and drowned in the process. Or maybe you're trying to get up enough nerve to try your luck. Whatever, we'll concentrate on the three limits I just laid out.

I hate the phrase "a friendly little poker game." I do not play friendly little poker and with all due respect, I don't think you should either. Note: This does not include my opinion of a friendly little game of strip poker, especially with the opposite sex, chosen from an elite group from the local modeling agency. In that game you are encouraged to lie, cheat, and revert to every conceivable method to relieve your opponents of their wares (clothes).

But in the real world of seven-card stud you'd better be alert, cautious, aggressive, cunning, and attentive—all at the same time. During the course of a seven-card stud poker game, every player gets approximately the same number of good hands and bad hands. The good player knows how to take advantage of good hands and how to get out of playing with lousy cards. The bad player does not know how to take advantage of good hands nor when to fold bad hands.

Therein lies the complete difference between a good or bad player.

Getting a great hand has to be cultivated so you get the most out of the pot. Knowing how to be patient and when to bang up, or raise, your bet is a key part of extracting the most from other players when you are sitting in fat city with a powerful hand. Knowing when to fold or cut losses in a poker game is an art. Those chips that a bad player tosses into the pot because it's "only a buck" or "I'll just take one more look" can add up to serious money during the course of a night.

Sometimes, popping a lousy buck into a pot to take one more card can leave you holding a mediocre hand, cause you to stay longer, and cost you money. A bad hand that is not folded and becomes a mediocre hand will prove expensive: The reason is you didn't have the guts to drop or were intimidated into taking another card because you felt other players would think you cheap for dropping out. Much more on this later, but understand that the silly little mistakes you make in a poker session can multiply into heavy losses.

Learn how to use good hands to their maximum benefit and when to throw in your cards when you're obviously third or fourth best. Sometimes you'll toss in a hand that a guy bluffed you into folding. Then you need to watch how that player performs or look for his "tells."

What's a tell? It's a BIG part of playing seven-card stud.

8

Tells

Might as well get to a chapter where you're gonna end up confused because you can't tell a tell from a tell. Let's start from the beginning. What is a tell?

A tell is a move a poker player will make that gives a hint as to what he is holding. Novice poker players are loaded with tells. They practically spit out whether they are weak or strong, on the come, bluffing, or sitting fat.

A good player looks for tells and exploits them. However, as you move up the ladder of poker playing and the opponents become more dangerous and the pots grow larger, a sharp player can give out a tell that is not really a tell. He's hoping you will assume it is a tell and then he will try to bang it back in your face. He is setting you up and it is your job to determine which is a tell and which isn't.

Poor poker players exhibit tells all night long and can't stop themselves. Over and over you'll hear a constant loser moan about his rotten luck and lousy cards. He checks his first three cards and visibly shows his disgust if he is dealt three clunkers.

The other night I played with a friend of mine, Juan Morshott. At one point, he stared at his three cards and disgustedly flipped his chip into the pot, moaning to himself, "One more shot, then I'm done. I just want to see one more card." Right away, I knew he was weak. He was really chasing at this point and shot his mouth off, begging for help from the next draw. When I had a decent hand against him, I banged up a larger bet to see if he would drop.

This was all brought about by listening to Juan Morshott complain after his initial three or four cards. Usually a guy on a losing streak slams his hand on the table when he drops out after suffering four, five, or six consecutive lousy starting cards. He is "telling" you he has poor cards. Then when he does remain in a hand, you know he has something. He is telling you he now has a competing hand.

Many, many times I'll fold a pair or even two pair when I see this complainer finally stay in a hand. He has shown a pattern of dropping out so continuously that when he does stay in, I fold, obviously not wanting to take on a guy who is probably stacked.

But, and here is the important part, you must observe what this guy does throughout that hand to see if, in fact, he was loaded. If he eventually drops out, your tell was premature and you lock that fact in the back of our mind. Wait and see if he ends up having to show his hand at the end, so you can get a strong read on him. Maybe he was just using a reverse play. A player who is suddenly screaming for someone to bet could be sitting in a strong position and is anxious for the game to proceed. In the end, I look to see if he really was sitting strong.

A player staring at the other players' cards on the table and hesitating before making his call could be on the "come" and not sure if he should stay in. That's a tell. The biggest tell is a tight player who constantly tosses in his hand after looking at his first three cards. He is content to stay in only when he is sitting strong after three cards. We'll get into offsetting this type of streak in an upcoming chapter.

There are certain players that bluff constantly. This is not a tell factor, but you must learn to read when a strong player bangs in a raise. Is it only when he is strong or is it usually in a come situation? This is a big point in picking up tells.

Some players will fold then jump up to grab a soda or sandwich instead of waiting to see how a hand develops and how each player reacts. I sit and watch what happens to the guy making the raise. Does he end up with a strong hand that may mean he became strong early and went right for the kill? Or does he eventually fold or lose, which indicates he will raise on the come? This is a tough guy to read, but his tell is that he is tough to get a handle on. All these things are tells and you must learn how to take advantage of them.

In low-limit games, you'll find guys with short or scared bankrolls. These players are more apt to display tells.

Spotting tells is a major part of poker playing. The next chapter pinpoints certain players and the need to get a read on them. Read it so you don't fall into a position of someone getting a read on you!

9

Reading the Players

A few years ago I made a videotape on seven-card stud. It is one of twenty-three gambling videos I've made and was by far the hardest to do, just as writing a book on poker is so difficult because there are so many intangibles to cover and so many variables. Or have I said this before?

Anyhow, here is how we made that tape. We asked for and received applications from people who wanted to appear on the video, and the only requirement was that they were experienced poker players. Again, the intent was to teach poker players how to refine their game, NOT to teach them how to play poker.

We settled on six guys and one woman. The day of the shoot, the seven players sat around a table. I walked over, opened a new deck of cards, shuffled the deck, and dealt three cards to each player, starting a hand of seven-card stud. Notice I did not set up hands to explain what to do. Each player was to decide what to do as the betting progressed. We dealt fourth street, then fifth street, stopping along the way to ask each player to comment on what he or she would do in each situation based on the cards they were dealt and how the betting was going.

Before the tape rolled, I had not had one single word with any of the players. Yet after four or five hands I could read the aggressive or conservative or erratic moves of each player. The point I was trying to make to them was that each was kicking off tells, not playing consistently, or most important, staying too long with weak hands.

When we completed the tape, they all admitted I concentrated more on reading the players' patterns than on simply playing my cards versus the high card or high hand on the table. I still recall telling that group the single flaw each of them had was failing to try and ascertain the moves of the players making bets.

To become a strong, successful poker player, you gotta follow the simple message in that old gambling song: "You gotta know when to hold 'em, know when to fold 'em."

Folding a decent hand based on the table bets or the bets of the previous two or three players, takes a lot of nerve and brains and logic. Sometimes it'll cost you a hand, but more times than not you'll end up saving a fistful of dollars.

On third street you're dealt a pair of 6s in the hole and a queen up. The player to your left opens for a dollar and is raised by a king, who in turn is raised by the 10. Your call is $3 or fold. With three cards dealt, the hand is 43 percent over and you're facing a potential raise-a-thon between at least two of the enemy. Even without getting into the tell factor, you have to fold. Sure, you're aware that one of the raisers is a habitual banger, but almost halfway to the finish line, you have a weak horse. Get out!

Now comes the hard job. You MUST sit and analyze that entire hand and watch for the outcome: Were either of these raisers bluffing? Did they eventually fold after one more card? Were they powerful at the end or simply betting on the come? Naturally, one hand will not unveil another player's entire bag of tricks, but the hands you encounter allow you the opportunity to get a read on the competition.

In that video, I stressed the need to pick up these patterns and even zero in on how long it takes a player to call or drop, all the way down to his method of throwing chips into the pot. Was he hesitant? Was he trying to decide whether to chance it or not? Was he looking around at the players after him to see if they had picked up their chips? Did he mutter anything that could give you a clue he was thinking any of the following: "ahh, one more shot" or "here's my donation" or "what's one more buck?"

These are tells. These are basic steps to follow to get an inkling of the patterns and moves of other players. Maybe most of them won't reveal anything at all. But if just one player does something you pick up on, you can use it against him down the road. It may help you win a hand or it may help you save money.

One thing is for sure: It can't hurt you to know your enemy. The big thing in poker is to learn to read the opposition.

10

Why Do You Play Poker?

If it took you more than a half a second to answer that question, you're barking up the wrong dog. I play poker for money and the thrill of the chase. On second thought, I play poker for money. If you have another reason, I'd sure like to hear it.

The messages in all my books and videos are geared to showing you how to cut losses (save money) and how to take advantage of streaks (make money). The messages in this book are pointed in the same direction. I assume you bought this book to see if I could help you along these financial lines.

Of course, some of you probably purchased this book (or borrowed it because you're too cheap to buy it) for the express purpose of getting tips from my excellent use of the inglesh langwich and perfeck grandma in describing farious sittuasions. But mostly you wanna know how to make money at poker.

Last week a friend of mine who is a floor person in one of the Atlantic City casinos was telling me she plays $1–$3 poker in the various poker rooms but feels bad when she takes another person's money. She said it doesn't give her any satisfaction to beat those players and that even when she loses $100 or so, she doesn't feel bad. I told her she had to be nuts. She figured she didn't have the mental toughness to succeed at poker. I agree. She is obviously out of her element if she thinks sitting around a poker table where real money is being wagered is strictly for fun. I suggested perhaps she take up softer pastimes like cleaning the tops of skyscrapers with a toothbrush and no net.

Poker, in my opinion, is a master battle of wits between

equally strong contestants. How you play the cards you are dealt is the determining factor in the outcome. Occasionally, you'll find a "patsy" or "fish" at your table. Make him pay. Find his weakness and attack him until you get him out of the game.

Years ago we had a Tuesday night poker game among a group of guys that had been together for years. We all knew each other's moves and exploited them. One fellow, his name was Al, was a schoolteacher and one of the nicest guys in the group, but he was a lousy player. He had more tells than a family of finks and used most of them every hand. He constantly dropped out after four cards until he had a strong hand. When he did bet, we all dropped so he ended up with the ante and a handful of coins. He never won a big pot. If I was exceptionally strong after four cards, I'd raise him to the limit until he finally went broke, which was never more than two hours into the game.

I truly liked Al and had absolutely no reason to go after him except for the money. When those cards were dealt, Al was my mortal enemy. Eventually, he stopped coming, after which time I zeroed in on Mike K., a fellow ball player who cried crocodile tears every single hand. He became the target of my attacks because he also had a ton of tells.

There are eight million stories in the naked city and eight million lousy poker players dying to be fleeced. I've told two of those stories. But the list goes on and on. Find the weakness in a player and bury him.

Maybe it sounds heartless, but that's the way the ding dongs. I play poker for money—yours. If you can beat me, I'll avoid you. But if you show me your weakness, I'll go after you. That's one of the things that helps me get your money. And money is the reason I play poker.

11

Reading the Cards

We talked about reading people, now let's get to reading the cards. In seven-card stud you get to see the up card and that's all. The other two cards are staring at the table top so they won't do you any good.

I check out my hand to see if it is worth a call (if I'm not the forced opener), then check out the six or seven up cards to see if there might be something I need. There ain't much you can do other than predetermining when you stay or drop. This is the first and probably biggest decision you need to make because it determines if you are strong enough to compete.

The only hand I can completely read is my own, so that is step number one. Let's say I am dealt a pair of 10s and a nonsuited jack. Naturally, I'm in unless another 10 shows on that board. Yeah, I fold my decent set of 10s as soon as I see another 10 staring back at me. With approximately twenty-one cards being dealt, that leaves only one 10 in thirty-two cards left for me to get trips, or three of a kind. My chances for getting that 10 diminish the more players there are. When you have five or more players staying after the initial third street, it stands to reason one or two of them have a pair. A good player stays in only if he does not see a mate to his pair on board. So you have maybe two opponents with a pair after third street and two of thirty-two chances of getting trips. But if you see one of your 10s on board, you now have only one chance in thirty-two of getting your trips. You fold your tens.

Reading people and catching their flaws is important. Reading the cards and ascertaining your chances of improving your pair is also important. Chasing that third 10 when there are two unaccounted is rough. Chasing that third 10 when there is only one left is crazy. Folding those 10s is hard to do, but it is necessitated by logic, the second of the Little Three.

Go a step further. Let's say you do not see a third 10 on the board after third street. You call and wait for your next card. You get a queen to go with your jack and pair of 10s. You feel good. A quick glance around the board and there sits 10 number three. You feel lousy. A quick math review reveals four of your seven cards are dealt. Fifty-seven percent of the hand is over and only one 10 is unaccounted for with twenty-six or twenty-seven cards to go. Not good odds.

The betting starts. A king checks but a 9 and 4 suited clubs bangs in a buck. No other raises but two calls bring the decision to you. Only two other clubs are accounted for around the table. You gotta drop. Sure, that club flush is on the come, but why is he coming out with a teaser bet? Either he's paired or has four clubs. If my third 10 is unaccounted for, I call the bet. If my third 10 is showing, I'm gone.

You cannot win every hand, but you also cannot stay every hand. Having the ability to read both the players and the cards is all you have going for you. Use that ability to cut your losses.

Remember, the checked king is still waiting to make his move and his raise may spur another raise from the possible club flush. If that third 10 is on the board, I'm gone. I'd stay if both 10s were unaccounted for and drop in all other instances. It's rough, but with five players hanging around at fourth street, it's time to run.

Learn to read the cards both from the standpoint of whether those you need are used up and also in terms of the potential power of the bettor in relation to your hand. Both those factors should be addressed before you call or drop.

12

Percentages in Poker

Man, how I hate to write this chapter. I truly hate trying to set a percentage on the odds of something happening or looking at charts people put in their books to show the possibility of pulling a "gut" straight on sixth street when one or two of the cards you need are already accounted for. My answer? Not good! Break it into percentages for you? I can't, I don't know how, and what difference does it make anyway?

It's a lousy move going for a gut or inside straight and that still doesn't guarantee a win. Yet inevitably some guy will ask me to give him a breakdown on what his chances are based on whether it's early or late in the game, cards dealt, position, and fourteen other stupid variables.

It's like my friend I. M. Madork asked after he had a bad day at the tables and decided to take a swan dive out a hotel window: "Hey John, what are my chances of survival if I dive from the eighth floor as opposed to the tenth floor?" I told him it depends on which direction the wind is blowing. He nodded like he believed me and went out to check the wind.

But I gotta write a chapter on this subject because it comes up all the time. The truth is I really don't care what percentages are involved because a bad move is a bad move is a bad move.

I never go for gut straights, and while we're on the subject of straights, I might as well give you another tidbit that will leave the so-called experts screaming I don't know what I'm talking about.

You're in a seven-card stud game with four players left on fifth

27

street, and you're sitting on 10, J, Q, K nonsuited and a 5 of hearts. This means no three cards are of the same suit, so all you have going is an open-end straight. A pair of 8s bets $5 and is called by a pair of 3s. A possible flush folds and it's up to you. Do you call, raise, or drop?

I fold and let the hate mail pour in.

To really get your dander up, let me also state that no 9s or aces have shown, so in effect the computer geniuses would scream that your chances of catching the open-end straight have increased. Increased to what? The odds of catching it are still against you, and even if you do catch the straight, you have two other hands to cope with. If one of those hands ends up with a flush or full boat, it's gonna be an expensive trip to the end of the line. The betting always intensifies on sixth and seventh streets, and my opinion is that straights don't hold up often enough to make up for the bets you lose chasing them.

You wanna chase straights? Be my guest, but unless I am dealt five cards in a row giving me that run, only a check at fifth street will let me stay and go for that overrated prize.

Back to percentages. A poker move should be based on either setting up a player, establishing a bluff, or going after a flush or higher hand. You're looking for value for your potential win. But poor percentage moves vary based on what cards are played and taking into consideration the down cards you can't see. Even if you are a newcomer to poker, a logical approach to going for a stronger hand is easier to comprehend than percentages.

Say you're through fifth street and hold Q, 10, 8, 5 of diamonds and a 5 of clubs. You're looking for help from the other nine diamonds. But spread out over the other six players' up cards are six diamonds you can see. That leaves only three unaccounted for with a bevy of down cards and two more draws. Betting on the table is heavy between a pair of 10s and a pair of queens.

Percentages be hanged: I'm running like a rabbit. Small chance of grabbing the diamond, and already two guys are building up the pot. Logic tells me my chances are weak to catch and suspect even if I do. Hang the percentage chart—

there's not sense gambling good money on the come. Another hand is coming up soon and maybe I'll be stronger in that one.

It was out in Las Vegas in the 1960s when I first got a taste of real poker. Then came the riverboats that had to travel five miles from shore to permit gambling. In those days, people couldn't even spell percentages but they knew a bad move from a good one. They used logical reasoning. It is a "feel" you'll get when you get serious about poker. It has to do with reading the players and the cards. Or have I said that before?

For years I was the victim, along with all the other green-horns who thought their booklearning and figures would carry them to the pot of gold at the end of each hand. Percentages in drawing a certain card? I'm not too good with the actual numerical situation, but I know when I'm in over my head and the best course of action is to fold. It's called LOGIC!

And logic is sure easier to spell—and understand—than percentages.

13

Wrapping Up the Introduction

It's time to wrap up this initial part of the book, but I hope you got an idea what I'm trying to convey about playing winning poker. There are some strong suggestions in the first few chapters, so it doesn't hurt for you to get back and zero in on some of the concepts. I don't want to repeat them here, but you'll know which areas I want you to concentrate on more than others. Reading players, reading and keeping track of played cards, cutting losses, and making logical moves make up the foundation of your preparation in playing winning poker. Absorb as much as you can.

Each of the next four sections covers a part of the Big Four, and special emphasis will be placed on the impact of the Little Three on your method of play. We'll start with bankroll, and when we get to the knowledge section, we'll go over moves to make at each step of seven-card stud, hi/lo, and Texas Hold 'Em.

But all the knowledge of what to do during a session will be for naught if you don't have money management and discipline. We'll get to those areas in due time, but for the moment just digest the things we've already gone over. I told you many of my theories are contrary to what you've heard or know about poker.

But unless you're kicking off a consistent return (regardless of the dollar amount) each week from poker, maybe it's time to try a new approach.

Just like effective medicine: Maybe you won't like the taste, but it will cure your ills.

Bankroll

14

Bankroll: The Start

The first of the Big Four is the bankroll, the amount of money you bring to the table or casino. Every single monetary decision you make is based on your personal bankroll.

A bankroll does not have to be gigantic. My friend Lee Till Short is a little short on cash and is embarrassed. He thinks unless you walk up to a table with $500 in your pocket, you're a pauper. Many people have that same misconception. Lee Till will say: "I'm a little short. I only have $300."

Only $300? That's more than enough to buy in at any $1, $3, or $1–$5 stud game, any $3–$6 game, and even a $5–$10 table. Bankroll does not mean big. It merely means the amount of money you bring to the battle.

From your bankroll, I want you to set loss limits and win goals. Reread the previous sentence 43,627 times and grasp what I have said, especially the two words beginning with the letter *L*. Failing to set win goals and loss limits destroys 90 percent of the people who gamble. (I'll illustrate the meanings of these two terms in subsequent chapters.)

It all comes down to this: Cut your losses to the bone and accept small wins! If you won't, you don't realize the power of setting limits. You wanna win the east wing of the casino, so you won't set a win goal. You won't quit until you lose every dime you have plus those you find near the slot machines.

Suppose you have $200 and enter a casino looking for a $1–$5 game. There is nothing wrong with buying in for $50 or $60. Most casinos have a rule called all in, so you never need to risk

33

more than your buy-in at that first game or session. The higher your bankroll, the higher stake you can play. But many professional poker players buy in with $60, $80, or even $100 in a $3–$6 or $5–$10 game.

I assume I am talking mostly to intermediate players right now, so I'll zero in on a $60 buy-in at a $1–$5 table.

You enter a casino with $200, peel off $60, and buy in at a $1–$5 game. Sixty dollars is about one-third of your total bankroll of $200, but you never take your entire amount to the first session. (This is covered in the next chapter, so bear with me.) You're keeping the balance of your bankroll socked away in case you have a bad run at this table or session.

Speaking of sessions, let's zero in on exactly what they are.

15

Sessions

A bad poker player will enter a casino, sit at a table, get lousy cards most of the night, and lose by a freckle when he finally gets a good hand. Another night this dork will get good hands, yet will constantly be beaten by players whose hands are just a notch better than his. In both instances, he will stay at that table, pouring good money after bad. Why won't he leave that table? Why doesn't he realize this is just not his night?

Years ago, when Maverick and Doc Holiday and all the other poker heroes of my childhood were sitting in saloons, glued to a poker table, it was usually the only game in town. They had to stay at one table or else go out and walk their horse. The same is true for your Friday night poker game where the same seven or eight guys huddle around the kitchen table for a game of straight, wild, and wilder poker. If you're having a bad night, you either suck it up and accept the loss or go home and watch another *Honeymooners* rerun. You stay because it's the only game in town.

But it's not that way in the casinos.

Casinos have lots of tables to choose from, and even if you have to put your name on a waiting list for an hour or so, at least you won't sit and get your clock cleaned, suffering through bad hands and bad luck. If you're gonna get serious about poker, you'd better be prepared to wear out your shoes walking from game to game until you find a decent table.

Every time you enter a game it is called a session. And each session should use an equal portion of your bankroll and have its own set of win goals and loss limits. As we discussed, the money you take into battle is your bankroll, which is broken down into sessions allowing you several shots during the course of a day. Here are some suggestions. First, let's look at a $1–$3 or $1–$5 game:

Bankroll	Number of Sessions	Buy-In
$200	4	$50
$210	3	$70
$300	4	$75
$500	5	$100

Note that your buy-in was very low when you got involved in an all-in game in the casinos.

Now let's look at a $3–$6 game:

Bankroll	Number of Sessions	Buy-In
$300	3	$100
$500	4	$125
$700	5	$140

There is no need to go higher than a $140 buy-in because you must protect that bankroll.

Finally, we'll take a short look at a $5–$10 game:

Bankroll	Number of Sessions	Buy-In
$600	4	$150
$600	5	$120
$1,000	5	$200
$1,000	4	$250

A $200 buy-in at a $5–$10 game is about right, although some players feel a higher stake makes them more comfortable. I prefer a lower buy-in because it restricts my losses and that, in my opinion, is the real key to gambling. Get into the habit of dividing your bankroll into equal sessions and making your buy-in an amount with which you're comfortable.

16

Loss Limits

Speaking of loss limits, this is the most important chapter in the entire book—bar none.

The key to gambling is cutting losses so you'll have a bankroll to allow you to enter the next battle. No matter how good you are, if you don't have money, you can't compete. I'm a great poker player, yet there are nights I get beat by being second best, or by simply not getting good cards. No matter how good you are, if you don't have the horse, you can't win the race.

I strongly subscribe to the idea of moving from table to table, setting loss limits along the way. When I enter the game, I surely wanna win as much as I can. But it is more important that I cut losses. Perhaps some of you will recognize this sentence: It's not how much you win that counts, it's how little you lose. Remember that message! I mention it in every book, video, lecture, or TV show I do. It is my main guide.

What is a loss limit per session? Glad you asked because it is much different than for table games.

Of the ten books I've written, the best by far is *Advanced Craps*, with *Sports Handicapping* a close second. There were more than five hundred pages in each of these books. No fewer than thirty-six chapters combined were devoted to cutting losses, minimizing losses, loss limits, accepting small returns, learning how to walk away, etc. Both books emphasized setting loss limits on the money you bring to a table or game as the key to betting.

Let's say $500 was your buy-in at a craps table. A hard-and-fast 50 percent of that $500 was your absolute maximum loss at that session. You would walk away with at least $250 in hand, thereby preventing the psychological trauma of being wiped out. In craps you need a decent bankroll to stay alive for several shooters, hence the $500 buy-in for a $10 bettor. But a 50 percent loss limit or lower is suggested. My loss limit is 30 percent with a $500 craps buy-in.

In poker I have already built in the loss limit by restricting your buy-in to only a small part of your total bankroll. You have more control over your chips in poker, betting only when you're in a strong or fairly strong position. In craps, blackjack, and the other games, you put your money on the layout and wait to see if you win or lose it all. Poker gives you options of cutting back or getting out of the hand altogether. That's why your loss limit in poker is your buy-in, and that's why I set up low buy-ins. You can play down to your last chip, as in the case of an all-in hand and still the loss is not devastating—IF you bought in for a small percentage of your total bankroll.

My friend Gofer Pott wants to win every hand, every big pot he gets involved in. He vehemently disagrees with my theory. Of course, Gofer Pott is usually broke but refuses to change his method of play. He takes his entire $400 bankroll to the first table and lets it all hang out. Usually, he'll find himself on the short end of a couple of strong players and end up hanging out at the bar until his ride takes him back home.

I've built in your loss limits and hope you'll realize the importance of holding down losses. Do I think you'll listen to this advice? No way. No way will you listen. What a pity!

17

Win Goals

Almost as important as loss limits are win goals, but only because they consist of a definite figure to shoot for in your sessions.

Sometimes a player will sit at a poker table for hours and hours. If someone asks him how long he plans to play, he'll usually look at his watch before he answers. He is not playing to win a certain amount of money—he is playing for a certain length of time, either until his bus leaves or his wife comes to get him.

I want you to set a win goal to shoot for, much like the loss limit that restricts how much money you can lose before wrapping up a certain session.

Suppose you bought in with $100 at a $1–$5 table and caught a nice run of cards. When you sat down you made a silent promise not to cheat on your wife for two weeks if you could just win $75. You catch a streak and soon you've got a nice $180 profit in front of you, and it took only one hour. But you never abide by that win goal—a barometer to determine when you'll slide a guaranteed profit aside while still playing with the excess. (I'll explain guarantee and excess in a moment.) A losing streak could sap that profit in no time and you could wind up giving everything back.

I want you to set a win goal. But that DOES NOT mean you're gonna have to leave the table when you reach your goal. It merely means that when you do reach your goal, you will make the smartest move of your life: rat-hole your starting buy-in and break your profit in half. Let's say it's $100. You put half ($50) in your pocket, not to be touched again at that session. The half you put aside is your guarantee, but the other half—$50 excess—allows you to continue to play.

Guarantee and excess are explained in detail in the money management section, so don't worry about retaining all this information if you haven't grasped the theory yet. But do understand that you MUST set a loss limit, which could be your total buy-in, but not one penny more. Your win goal could be anywhere from 60 percent to 100 percent of your buy-in before you put the guarantee and excess into operation.

You'll still be playing at that table, but it'll be a comfortable feeling knowing you socked away a profit that ensures you'll leave that session with more money than you started with. The amount of your win, whether it be big or small, is absolutely, positively unimportant. Sometimes you have to accept small returns. But it sure beats no return at all.

One final note: Don't make a boob of yourself by setting a win goal three times the amount of your buy-in. It'd be too difficult to reach, and I want you to get into the habit of taking something of a profit each session, or at least most of the time.

Will you listen to this advice? Probably not. But someday you'll realize white man does not speak with forked tongue. I just hope it ain't too late for you to get into the habit of winning.

18

Short Bankroll

Here's a malady that affects most people who gamble: the short bankroll. That means you're operating with money you should be putting into more important things.

My friend Shorty Shortkash is a little short of bread, but still he wants to play poker to grab a few dollars. He owes $600 rent, which is due in four days. He has $200 and figures everything will be honky-dory if he gets into a card game and wins $400.

Does he get into a $1–$3 poker game where the lower stakes will keep him solvent for a longer period of time? No way. This mental midget plops into a $10–$20 game and lasts about twenty minutes until he gets sucked into a heavy pot where he must stay with his trip deuces. Eventually he goes all in, catches a pair of queens for his small boat, then is shocked back to reality when some cat fills his two pairs of 10s and 9s. Our hero is dead in the water. He played too short in a game totally out of his bankroll realm. Now he doesn't even have a leg up on getting back into action. He played short and in the wrong game.

You think there aren't thousands of people playing in games every day with a short bankroll? It happens all the time—and then some.

If you are down on your financial stepladder, don't play until you can play comfortably. If you do get involved with a short bankroll, at least have the brains to get into the absolutely lowest game you can find. I'm talking 25¢, 50¢, or at best, $1–$3 tables. Even then you're nuts!

Don't play short. If you do, you'll play scared. If you play scared, you'll play dumb, and you know what happens when you play dumb.

19

Scared Bankroll

This is in the same pew as the short bankroll. In this case you are gambling with money you borrowed, stole, or had earmarked for fairly important purchases like shoes for the kids or food for the fridge. Instead of using the money for necessary items, you pocket the dough and head for the casinos and a game of Texas Hold 'Em.

In the back of your mind you realize what a dingdong you are and that if you do blow the wad, you'll be facing the commander of the teepee—your wife—who will want a detailed report on where her food money is. But even though you know she is waiting in the wings back home, you still decide to take your shot. The mind is willing but the discipline is weak. You're constantly thinking of the consequences should you lose. You're playing scared.

One of the biggest tells at a table is the scared player. He counts his chips constantly, fumbles when he hears the word *raise,* checks decent hands all the time, and acts like a frustrated teenager being turned down for his junior prom. Every loss drives him into soft curses, wild looks at the winning player, and an outright show of agitation, regardless of whether he has a good or bad hand. He never takes a chance and constantly plays timid.

There is absolutely NOTHING wrong with a player hating to lose. Even the best go belly-up certain days. That's why they call it gambling. But if you're playing scared or playing with scared money, back off and wait until you're financially sound and mentally tough. There are rotten, lousy punks like me who'll pick up on your tenseness and make you pay. It ain't worth it!

20

Wrapping Up Bankroll

There are a lot of messages I could give you about having the proper bankroll, but the words would just pass through, over, and around the block of empty granite that sits on your neck. That's because people don't realize the importance of all four parts of the Big Four. They think that because they know all the right moves in poker, can pronounce money management in six languages, and can spell enilpicsid backward they have the right to play poker or get involved in any gambling endeavor.

Well, the first of the Big Four is bankroll and too many people play scared, short, or stupid. Many times all three.

If you don't have money, you can't expect to be able to compete. I KNOW you need the money, but betting with a short bankroll is acceptable only if you'll accept small returns. You'll hand me all types of garbage as to why you gamble, but the real reason people gamble is for money. In fact, it's about 90 percent of the reason.

I love the chase and the challenge. I don't NEED the money to exist, but I mostly gamble for money and feel rotten when I lose. I am disgusted with myself, and yeah, I go back over each session to figure out what I did wrong.

So if you admit to being one of the 90 percent, why not try my theories? They have a logical approach for keeping you afloat until your trend pops up. Funny, the Little Three wormed their way into that message. Do you remember what they are?

Nowhere in this book will you find me telling you to have a great big bankroll to compete at poker. But you will find me constantly telling you to base your win goals on the size of your bankroll. Winning 50 percent of your day's bankroll will make you sleep comfortably and will result in a positive outlook for future games. Naturally, you must strictly adhere to your loss limit because you cannot win at every session. But you sure as heck can cut your losses and make the trek back from a losing day an easier chore.

It all starts with bankroll, regardless of its size. The more you have, the better and more relaxed you'll play. But whatever you have, set your win goals and loss limits on that amount.

Bankroll. It's the beginning. Next we move into knowledge of the game.

Stud

21

Seven-Card Stud

It is tough writing on knowledge of the game because the move variations change drastically every time a card is dealt, based on the players involved and the different methods of play. In my *Advanced Craps* book are 131 chapters on money management and thirty-two chapters on knowledge. That's because money management in gambling is head and shoulders above knowledge of the game.

Walk through a bookstore and you'll see volumes of information on playing poker written by different experts who are all excellent poker players. They offer a multitude of moves for every situation, and you start to bob and weave from all the information being tossed your way. It is absolutely impossible to give a hard-and-fast rule for something that arises game after game. That's because the decision to call, raise, check, check and raise, or drop changes constantly, depending on the players in the game, the betting up to that point, your position in the betting stage, and the moves generated on the previous street.

Once you become a poker player, the next step is perfecting your play to a point where you can read the other players' moves, bets, and patterns. And even that changes from hand to hand.

Then comes the art of deception in your play. You should spend a lot of time watching the moves of your opponents to pick up patterns of what they do in certain situations, then use this against them. By the same token, you must vary your moves to prevent the other strong players from picking up your patterns.

Let me give you an example: You're dealt AD, QD down, and 9D up. You call the minimum bet and the next card get a JD, giving you four diamonds, with more showing than anyone else. A pair of 6s bets $3 and you raise, letting your move suggest you have a higher pair, possible straight, or four-card flush. You get a couple of calls, eventually fill the flush, and win the hand. The sharp guys at the table make a mental note that you raised with a four-card flush on the come, so they give you a nod as aggressive, regardless of whether you won or lost the hand.

An hour later the same situation arises—5H, 10H in the hole, and JH up. You call on third street and get a QH, giving you four hearts with a possible straight or flush. A pair of 8s bets $3 and you are the final caller after four other calls. Do you raise as you did before, although this time two hearts are on board, or do you just call?

Without hesitation, you call, giving the wise guys zeroing in on your move the impression you are not sitting with four hearts since before you raised with a four suit. The exact same situation, different move. So what am I supposed to tell you is the "proper" move? I know doggone well I'm gonna play it the way I just laid it out to you. At the end of that hand the sharp players are gonna have a hard time getting a fix on my moves in a certain situation because of my flexibility. You can bet your house I'm gonna make sure the other players see I had four hearts early and still chose to call. If I fail to catch my flush, I can casually turn over my two down hearts to make sure the move is noted.

So I don't think I have the almighty right to say such and such a move is the correct one when thousands of situations arise in every game where the theories of the other players dictate what you should or should not do. I will give you my theory and let you decide if you wanna adopt it. Again, I am talking to intermediate players looking to jump a step in their game. I don't expect you to agree with all my theories, but take the ones that seem most logical and place them in a section of your head for reference during a game.

I am absolutely certain my words will bring sighs of disgust from authors who disagree vehemently with my method of play. As a great Irish philosopher once said, "Come Si, Come Sigh." Or something like that.

22

Casino: Seven-Card Stud Basic Rules

OK, let's go over how a typical casino parlor game is run. Just remember it may change a little in your local casino, riverboat, reservation casino, or whatever is available. But basically, we are dealing with universal rules. If you like, ask the dealer to go over the rules when you sit down. He'll know you are aware that there are ground rules.

There is usually a desk in front of the poker room where you give your name, game preference, and the limits you'd like to play. Here are a few you may have seen listed:

seven-card stud	$1–$3
seven-card stud	$1–$5
seven-card stud	$2–$4
seven-card stud	$3–$6
seven-card stud	$5–$10
seven-card stud	$10–$20
seven-card hi/lo (8)	$1–$3
seven-card hi/lo (8)	$3–$6
seven-card hi/lo (8)	$5–$10
seven-card hi/lo (no qual)	$10–$20
Texas Hold 'Em	$1–$3
Texas Hold 'Em	$2–$4
Texas Hold 'Em	$5–$10
Texas Hold 'Em	$10–$20
Texas Hold 'Em	$20–$40

Naturally, your card room might have other levels of play plus Omaha Hold 'Em and Omaha hi/lo (8). Then there are Pineapple and a lot of spin-off games popping up all over the place. Since I told you I was only gonna stay with seven-card stud, hi/lo, and Texas Hold 'Em in this book, that is all I listed.

So you check the board, pick your game, and sign the list. When there is an opening, you will be taken to that table. Let's say you're into a $1–$5 seven-card stud game. When you sit down, drop your session money on the table—we'll say it's $100. The dealer will give you chips totaling that amount in the form of $1 whites and $5 reds. At the same time he will explain the basic rules of the game—as a good dealer should!

Some games have antes, some do not. I strongly suggest a no-ante game, but take what your casino offers.

The dealer will explain the ante each player puts up before the deal, which at this level is about 25¢. Then he'll tell you the table gets a 5 percent take (rake) per hand, and whether there is a limit on what they'll take in the event of a big pot.

The dealer has absolutely no financial interest in the game. He is employed by the house to shuffle, deal, call out hands, take the rake, and judge each hand as to winner or split pot, which he divides equally among winning hands. A good dealer keeps the game flowing with little or no useless chatter. He is usually tipped each hand by the winner. In a $1–$5 game, a dollar is a normal tip. I've also seen 50¢, 25¢, 10¢, and plenty of times, no tip.

If you're not a tipper, so be it. It's not my place to tell you what a no-good, rotten, stinking cheapskate you are. Should you tip? Yes! How much? I throw a dollar at this level and a couple of chips in the higher games. But yes, you should tip.

The dealer shuffles and deals two cards down and one card up to each player, with the low card required to bet $1 to get something in the pot. Growing up we all played where the high card always bet first. But that only applies on fourth street and up. This way a dollar bet by the ace or king doesn't scare out the rocks.

A dollar is bet by the low card up and each player in turn

calls, drops, or raises. In turn means only after the player to your right makes his move do you make yours. This is a must in the game as it avoids arguments because some guy put his chip in too early, only to find three guys in front of him exercise raises. This guy can't and shouldn't get his premature bet back. So bet in turn.

The game continues until seventh street when the remaining players make their final bets, raises, and calls. There are three raises allowed except when it comes down to two players going head-to-head. Then there's no limit on raises. Check the rules at your game for clarification. When the last players complete the betting, all remaining hands are shown and the dealer calls out the winner and shovels the chips the winner's way. The dealer's rake, or drag, is done after each street is completed. He keeps the rake at his right until the game is over. Then he deposits it in the table slot.

There you have the basic rules. Nothing intimidating about that. In fact, you never have to speak.

23

Casino: Stud

Just in case you're a veteran poker player with the boys on Friday night and are new to the casino style, we'll go over a few things that may be new to you.

You're still gonna get the following:

jerk who raises every hand
talker who tells you what he has—and lies
boob who goes after female players because he thinks they don't belong in the game
stayer who NEVER goes out
outer who plays very, very few hands
tight player (see "outer")—also called a "rock"
idiot who wants to see the hands of players to his right or left
crier who complains after every hand that he has no luck or that God hates him
drunk who disrupts the game
ante-stealer who bumps constantly on third street, trying to grab antes and drive players out

It's unbelievable how many dorks there are at the tables. I personally get irritated by the dork who replays every hand and figures what each player would get if so and so hadn't dropped out or if this guy stayed and so on. When the hand is over, it's history. I don't wanna hear what woulda, coulda, shoulda happened, and if you're one of those people who rehashes every hand, forget it.

There's nothing wrong with some friendly talk at a table, but be sure you're ready with your bet when it's your turn. The losers sure don't wanna hear long stories or suggestions on how to keep their grass greener. If you're giving out personal phone numbers of the Playmate of the Month, well, that's another story. I'm a big listener in that area. But everything else is worthless chatter.

Yes, you can check and raise at the table and nobody is gonna shoot you. Maybe they won't like it, but it's a good move by strong players and is done all the time. Learn to use it because it's gonna be used on you. If you're sitting with the top hand of a pair of 3s on board with a third one in the hole, you're in a nice situation. You could be staring at a possible flush and straight, so there's nothing wrong with a check to see where the enemy stands. If he calls, you can be sure I'll come back with a raise, especially if we're on fifth or sixth street and he's still on the come.

There is also a rule in most games, which originated in Las Vegas: After the hand is completed, a player who dropped out early because of some back-and-forth raises can ask to see the cards of the players who stayed to the end. That player, even though he is not involved in the final plays, has the right to see those cards. This prohibits players from working as a team and getting involved in a bumping situation where the moves are designed to catch an unwary player in the middle of fake raises. If the winner shows a full house while his opponent shows a nonsuited 3D, 3C, 5C, 8H, 9H, QD, KS, it's obvious they were working together. This situation is brought to the attention of the poker room manager and he has the right to expel that player, or both players, or at least split them up. But yes, you can ask to see a player's hand even if you folded early.

You may hit a slight hitch at a table where you are losing with decent hands after a previously nice run. Ask for a plastic marker to hold your spot and take a walk for a spell. In other words, the table ain't killing you, but you may be going through a slightly bad trend. Take a short breather.

As we go along, I'll address team play and other things that could occur, but keep in mind that the switch from your kitchen table to the casino is not drastic. The house doesn't cheat and management tries to run 100 percent clean games.

24

Stud: Third Street

Let's go to the meat of a hand, and at this point in the book the messages you'll read are my own ways of playing. They might bring beads of sweat to the foreheads of experienced players whose methods differ from my theories. My approach is to read the other players for obvious flaws, memorize cards played, cut losses when I have lousy hands, and maximize profits when I'm in fat city with a strong hand.

Realize right off the bat that no matter how good you are, or think you are, you CANNOT win every hand. Why? I dunno, but it has something to do wit the big guy upstairs deciding you ain't so special that you are allowed to be king of the universe. It took me a long time to come to grips with this fact, and now I gladly settle for winning 10 percent of the hands I play. The trick is making bad hands eat up as small a chunk of my session money as possible. At the same time, if I do get a good shot at a winning hand, I want to maximize my win for that particular hand.

Keep in mind that in seven-card stud the average winning hand is probably in the neighborhood of three 9s. With that in mind, you can make a lot of money-saving decisions based on the competing players and their styles.

Your first real decision is based on the first three cards dealt, which we'll call third street. There used to be hard-and-fast rules for when to stay or drop after you examine these three cards since they represent about 43 percent of the cards you'll get in seven-card stud. My hard-and-fast stays are any pair and

56

three cards to a flush. Naturally, I am forced to stay with the low-card-must-bet rule now prevalent in all casino games. But these two hands are definite stays.

Then the offshoots take place. You're gonna run up against ante-stealers and guys who love to raise on the first three cards, sometimes merely to drive out players who like to play tight. As poker has become more and more popular, it has attracted more and more players with short bankrolls who can buy into a poker game with $40 and sit like rocks hand after hand. In a no-ante game, a rock can look at three cards hand after hand with no dollar risk and keep folding until he has a competing hand. In fact, in a $1–$3 or similar low-stake game, this rock can see his first three cards, and often his fourth card, for as little as a $1 investment.

This is not a complaint against these players. It is simply a fact and who is to say they're wrong? I've played in poker games where women brought their knitting and men listened to music through earphones, read newspapers, or brought snacks. This is not uncommon in low-stake games throughout the country where the players settle in for long sessions, short outlays of cash, and possible returns of a day's pay. Are these people wrong? Of course not.

They can and will wait out the player who gets antsy and anxious, dropping out hand after hand. The patient player waits for the antsy one to stay in when he is going on the come, fails to catch, and gets whacked by the rock who plays only when loaded or semiloaded.

You can decide which way to handle these first three cards, but I've shown you my standard stays.

Let's say you are dealt KC, QD, and JH. No flush showing but three high cards to a straight. I will stay if it costs me only a call, and there are only two or fewer hands that match my cards showing around the table. I am staying, not because I am thinking straight but because I wanna offset the thinking of a player trying to get a read on my moves on third street. If I see a combination of three or more cards matching my three high cards, I throw it in. That move was strictly to offset getting read as a rock while having three decent cards.

Let's suppose my first three are 8D, 9C, and 10H. I am gone. Why? I rarely win with a straight because I rarely go for one. I don't even consider the other cards on board when I am dealt three cards to a straight when they are low or medium. I'm gone.

If I win with a straight, it is by accident since I was probably looking to better a pair or flush. Straights are too tough to catch, so if I fall into one at fifth street in the process of going in another direction, I'll look like a sharp dude who pulled that straight. Truth is, I never go for them and that includes open straights on fourth street, unless three of those cards are suited.

This is my basic approach to third street. Next we swing into variables.

25

Variables: Third Street

You've heard the terms "poker face," "bluffing," "rat-holing," "conning," cutthroat," and several others used to describe people (like me) of rather unscrupulous actions.

Well, they all seem to be attached to the game of poker because if a move is associated with cheating, the phrases "dealing from the bottom of the deck," "dealing seconds," "false cuts," "stacking the deck," "card shark," and another handful of bad accusations are immediately aimed at the poker player.

I've been playing poker since television was just a dream, and I have heard every single one of these accusations. Whether they are true is another story. But the fact they struck so close to home and I didn't deny them indicates the caller was at least in the neighborhood of the callee's character.

These accusations go with the territory, but look at it from the perspective of the accused. It puts him in a position to use the implications in his favor. If you are labeled a straight player or rock, a bluff is picked up immediately. A raise is met with constant folds by the opposition. A card shark is assumed to be full of tricks. He can use a variety of moves to his advantage, sometimes causing the opponent to think two or three times before deciding if a move is real, imagined—or made to counteract the thinking of the thinker who may think the pro is doing something to offset the opposition or to make that player think he is doing something while all the while he is doing nothing yet making the other player get lost in attempting to decipher the move.

I want you to repeat that last sentence word for word, then explain it in detail. You'll be marked on penmanship and length because the true message is clear: A so-called card shark is in a position to confuse opponents.

I want you to have multiple moves, even at third street, to offset others getting a read as to your stay or drop. This is done by varying your moves on third street, depending on your cards and your position in relation to the betting process.

To avoid being detected as a rock, I'll call a bet when I have any two cards suited, as long as one of them is a J, Q, K, or A. A call would be 4D, 9S, KS, when there are only two or fewer spades on board. To me, that is a stronger play than 4D, 5H, 6C. I still need three spades, but there are still nine unaccounted for if two are showing on board.

Before I go deeper let me emphasize this move. It is NOT a constant thing. It is only done if I have had a bad run on my first three cards that forced my dropping several hands in a row. I need something to put out the impression that I am not a rock. Also, I must have at least one power card of that two-card suit, as long as there are no more than two additional cards of that suit on board.

Many players show too much of themselves on third street and drop constantly or make tells by slamming their cards down when they are trying to give the impression they don't wanna fold. This display of mock anger is not gonna get any sympathy from the other players.

Here are a few stays or drops:

any pair... stay
three-card flush... stay
K, J, 5, nonsuited... drop
AC, QC, 4D... stay
AD, 9D, 4H... stay

Stay only if you've been dropping a lot; occasionally call to offset a read.

Next chapter we'll touch on raises and moves when there are raises on third street.

26

Wrapping Up Third Street

Once you decide exactly which three cards you feel comfortable with from a standpoint of stay or drop, go back to the previous chapter and reread the description aimed at those of us who are unworthy of the title "gentleman of leisure," a description more acceptable than the obviously truer version I laid out for you. Therein lie the moves I want you to make to counteract those ante-stealers and sharpies that play aggressive on third street in order to force the hands of the rocks and tight players.

In Texas Hold 'Em the game is weighed heavily in favor of position. That means the last two players who bet after everybody else has made a decision are in a great position. These players utilize their right to bump and thereby chase anyone trying to last long enough to see a free flop. A seven-card stud player uses that same theory on third street, especially when he is in the final betting position. There are always tight players making a quick exit on third street. Then there are those willing to throw in a dollar call bet in order to see fourth street, giving them four cards for a buck.

If you're in the last seat, four players are still in, and you're really strong with your first three cards, there are a couple of schools of thought. Let's say you have three spades wired and none showing on board, or you're dealt a pair of kings down with a suited queen up and there is a bet and four calls. You are strong and can merely call. Or you can raise and cause a few drops or scare everyone out and forfeit your shot at a decent pot with a strong base.

Obviously you'll stay, but the key is to throw off your opponents. Let's say you raise $3, making everyone fold. Be sure you let the table see it was not a bluff. Throw your cards in face up, not to make them feel good that they got out but to give them something to think about: They know you'll raise on third street when you're strong.

Let's suppose you're dealt three cards suited with none on board, or a pair of queens with none on board, and there is a previous raise. I call because a second raise on third street would probably chase everyone else and leave you head-to-head with limited value even if you do win. Don't bluff on third street, trying to catch the ante or get a player to back off. It's a wasted bet. I'll raise on third street if I'm strong but never bluff that early.

If a rock raises on third street, I fold even if I'm strong. Occasionally a rock will raise and scare off a player with a decent pair or three cards suited, but you're not out any cash, so don't let it bother you. A tough move is folding on third street when you have a pair of 10s or better, none on board, only one high card showing, and two guys making raises. It's too early to see if they're legitimate, so I toss in my 10s. But as soon as possible, when you have a decent hand on third street, bang in your raise to make the point that you will kick the pot early so they can't get a fix on your play.

I keep harping on changing your play and this is important early in the game. As you go deeper into the hand, the moves are easier to make based on whether you are strong with good cards or are having a hand flatten out. In a nutshell, third street is a good place to confuse your opponents by altering your moves. Sometimes it'll cost you a pot when you chase a weak player when you are strong, but my intent is to set up my opponents for future hands.

I like to use my first three cards to make strong impressions. My moves have to make a statement. Vary that statement and let them see you are flexible.

27

Session Money

Before we get to fourth street, let me touch on something that will apply to a lot of people, especially in lower-limit games. It is a universal drawback for most people who play poker: You ain't got a healthy bankroll. We're not playing liar's poker in this chapter, we're baring our souls and touching on a situation most of us go through.

Do you think I didn't go through the weeks, months, years of tight, short, scared bankrolls? Did it affect my play? Of course it did. How could I say it didn't?

The guy raising and playing crazy is usually the guy on a hot roll. He has built up a nice pile or bought in with a healthy amount of cash. His moves are based on the scare tactics he uses to intimidate players with short or tight bankrolls. Players will fold in the face of these raises with hands that warrant a call or reraise. That's because a player with a tight bankroll doesn't play smart. His moves are made to counteract the fact that he is short of money and the deep-pocket player is throwing the game out of whack.

You're gonna get into these games where your decisions are affected by big, early, and seemingly constant irrational raises. If it is affecting your play or decisions, here is a list of the things you must do, even if you don't want to:

1. Play your hand and fight back, even though you're playing short.

2. Keep folding, hoping he'll eventually go broke.
3. Leave the table.

Obviously (3) is the right move and you must do it, but you probably won't. If you follow (2), you're nuts; you've played into his hands without taking advantage of the strong cards you're being dealt, so you've lost all power to counteract. You've lost control and the chance of competing sensibly. If you chose (1), it's only a matter of time before his bankroll will devour you. A person playing that way is only marking time, waiting to lose.

I know you're short of cash. That's why you're in a $1–$3 or $1–$5 game. The guy raising the table knows it and is banging away at the financial weaknesses of those players.

Which brings me back to telling you to have a proper bankroll and session amount. I am not condemning tight players who are forced to play like rocks because of financial drawbacks. But if you can't hold out until you are properly financed, you have to leave the tables where constant bettors and raisers are operating. They will take you completely out of your game.

I play with this type individual at different level games and they are irritating. But if you don't let their aggressive play work on you mentally, you can read their patterns and adjust your play. It comes down to positioning your rebetting and raising tactics when you have strong cards. Play smart, know when to raise, and avoid being intimidated into making quick drops or dumb moves because of your lack of money.

As we move into the latter streets of a game, I will assume you have the session money to play intelligently. You don't have to buy into a session with the family jewels, but you gotta be able to operate freely... and smartly. Bad grammar, good advice!

28

Fourth Street

There's a lot to be aware of on fourth street. We know no one has a straight, flush, or full house. A pair could be four of a kind, but that is so unbelievably rare the worst we're facing is trips, a four-card straight, or a four flush. You know what you have, so now zero in on the competition, trying to remember who, if anyone, raised on third street.

First things first. Are you strong enough to stick around with your four cards? In my case a probable straight, a totally blah hand, or two-card flush is an automatic dive. That leaves the size of my pair or a three-card flush to keep me in. This is decided by the betting and where I stand in terms of calling and being raised by the players to my left. I don't mind the raise if I'm strong, but a small pair is courting trouble because even a call of a single raise puts me in a chasing pattern.

Naturally, you're gonna call with a pair of any kind, no others on board, and no raises. That's easy. Knowing the player or players to your left gives you an insight as to whether they are habitual raisers or kick it up only when they are strong. With no raises, I stay with a pair of 7s or better and none on board, regardless of where I'm sitting. I'll call a raise if I'm deep in the betting around the table and have a power pair and none showing.

If I have a power pair (J, Q, K, A) and three cards suited, I'll stick in a raise when there are two pair hands or fewer showing. I like to show I'll bet on the come. Fourth street is a good place to do this, especially when my pair is second best and only two of my suited cards are on board.

For example: My down cards are QD, 6D; my up cards QC, 8D. they could read me for a possible straight or high pair. If there is a habitual raiser, I'll raise if my two up cards are suited and I have a power pair. In this case I have QD, QC in the hole and 6D, 8D showing. So what if he reads me flushing—it'll slow down his raising. Get your opponent to try and read you, but my raise is only done this early if I have a couple of options working. The power pair or three suited cards give me two shots.

If the raiser comes back at me, I'll call, but my message was sent. If I am dealt a four-card flush and there are four or more showing, I'm calling on fourth street. They know you're not flushed this early and with no pair to back you up you're too easy to read.

I raise on fourth street when I've got shots going or to get a read on somebody I suspect is false-raising. Watch his face when you reraise him. If he comes right back with another raise, he's probably strong. If he stops and tries to figure out what you have and then just calls, he's usually on the come or looking to bang somebody out. If I have trips on fourth street, raise a raise, and get reraised, I don't have any raises left, but I now know where my competition is.

I'm not gonna give you three thousand examples of hands because you'll eventually acquire the feel of the game. But I will emphasize that you concentrate on player traits:

Zero in on the rocks.

Zero in on scared or short bankrolls.

Get a fix on big raisers at the table by checking out their hands when the last cards are shown. If they constantly raise on fourth and fifth streets and are not strong on seventh, they're constantly on the come.

At fourth street be sure you're not suckered in with one lousy pair and stuck for raises.

Don't make a habit of raising on fourth street, but when you're strong, don't hesitate to raise.

A lot of bad players stay through fourth street with weak hands. That's a no-no!

29

Fourth Street Fallacies

You've heard the phrase "When you're strong, keep the suckers in, don't raise them out." I think that is a stupid approach to playing poker. There is such a thing as allowing someone to draw out on you by keeping him involved. Who knows which approach is better? In a situation where my hand is showing trips on fourth street, I want that pot, regardless of how little or how much is in it.

If I'm dealt trips wired, I call on third street, but on fourth my palms get itchy to have chips—someone else's—in my hands. When my pair is shown, I bet the max. If you're gonna beat me, you'll have to pay for the right. When the trips are hidden, I raise the max, giving my opponents something to think about. In other words, I bang it on fourth street with trips.

There is a big emphatic NO when it comes to sucking the players along, trying to build a pot. The best laid plans of mice and men, etc. What's so wrong with playing strong when you are strong?

When you check your trips on fourth street or even call a bet, you're inviting the flush and straight players to improve. The same is true with two pairs or four cards to a flush. I am gonna get as many people out as I can with maximum bets and raises.

Let's look at having trips or a four-card flush and raising the first bettor. I am then raised by either a higher card than my trips are or a two-card flush. I've already got my power start and the raiser may be merely checking me out. I'll reraise immediately to send the message I am ready to go all the way. But now I know where the competition is. It's obvious he doesn't have a straight or flush, and depending on what my high flush card is, we're pretty even going in.

Raising on fourth street when you're strong is not a bad move because it's fairly easy to read the competition's hand. But if I'm sitting with a single pair on fourth street, between two raises, and at least one has two suited cards showing, I'm gone. Maybe it's a premature drop because I could improve, but I have to assume one of these raisers has something.

Aggressive players do a lot of raising on fourth street, trying to scare off the hangers-on. I'll stay with a high pair for a call, but won't chase two raisers even if one has shown he's a habitual raiser. I'm still not strong enough to combat him, and 57 percent of the cards I'm going to get leave me sitting with only a lousy pair. If I have a four-card flush on fourth street with two raisers, will I stay? Yes, as long as no more than three of my flush cards are showing.

Fourth street is an excellent point to read the other players because you can see half their cards and compare them to your own hand. If you've mastered reading players, you'll know which direction they're going on this street.

Suppose I have a four-card straight at this point: 8H, 9C, 10C, JS. Will I stay? Only for a call, no raise. And only if I'm late in the betting with a small chance of raising in front of me. And no, the two clubs are not strong enough to entice thoughts of a flush. One raise and my potential straight is discarded. Sorry, I don't chase straights. Or have I said that before?

30

Wrapping Up Fourth Street

It ain't hard to wrap up this street because my financial input has been small, and to get past third street I must have had something. If I didn't improve with that fourth card, I run unless a check glides around the table. The fact that I reached fourth street and then improved means I can see a call or one raise. And if I really improved, I'll become the aggressor!

That's why it's important as early as possible to get a fix on which players make their moves, based on an aggressive move at this street or a wait-and-see stance.

I've already told you that if I'm strong, I use this street to raise and give a message that I've got something, either four flush, trips, or two pairs. Then a reraise can't hurt me. The absolute worst thing that could happen at this point is having a high pair (queens, kings, aces) and face two raises from hands I perceive as going for a flush or possible trips. It takes guts to fold, but that is the proper move even if no matches to my pair are on board. If I do choose to fold at this point, it'll be hard for me to be labeled a "runner" after a raise as long as I play super aggressive on fourth street when I'm decent. Don't run all the time on fourth street. If you're strong, bang it in.

This is a nice position where your investment is small, you can see your potential based on your four cards, and you can start to get a read on your opponents. Bottom line: Don't be afraid to fold a single pair in the face of two raises. Don't be afraid to raise when you are sitting with a pair, trips, or a four-card flush.

I make my move on fourth street because on fifth street my decision to stay or fold becomes reality. I want to send a message before I get to numero five!

31

Fifth Street

Here's where they separate the men from the boys. Here's where I make my move to either go on or dive. Fifth street is decision time, and in seven-card stud, it is the pivotal part of the game for all players, or at least it should be. When you have your fifth card, 71 percent of the hand is finished. There are only two cards to go, and if you can read, you have a clear-cut read on your opponents.

A straight is self-explanatory, and since three cards are showing, you can get a fairly clear picture of every hand going in that direction. If the guy got his straight in five cards, you can bet he's gonna come on hard. One check or nonraise from him and I ignore him for the moment.

The possible flushes are the biggest problems. If a player doesn't have three suited cards showing, you know he doesn't have a flush. He could have four cards to a flush and be betting that way, but at least you know where that enemy stands.

Again, for me to get to fifth street, I probably have a good or decent hand or backed in with a lot of checks. If that's the case and I end up with one lousy pair and a raise comes up, I'm gone—period. Maybe he's bluffing, I don't care. This is my key change station and if I'm not strong, I get off and wait for the next train. More money is lost with bad hands on fifth and sixth street than at any other position. If I'm still in when the betting ends at fifth street, you'd better believe I've got something, unless I got a cheap ticket to sixth street with a series of checks, which means nobody is strong.

Once I ascertain the strength of my cards, I check out possible flushes and any pairs that may have surfaced in the other hands. If I don't have a straight at this point, I ain't looking to go on. But an open straight with a power pair (J, Q, K, A) will allow me to call a bet—not a raise. That may be hard to swallow, but at fifth street I have to assume one of the remaining players has something. Even if we all have just one pair, the chances are slim that I can outdraw three or four of them. Sure it could happen, but you gotta set up guidelines to follow and one pair this deep doesn't excite me.

A lot of theories have to do with making a raise on fifth street when you are last in the betting, have a pair, and note one bet and three calls in front of you. Let's say the last in the betting raises on his lousy pair. All of a sudden the player that bet or called bangs back a raise. Now you don't know if you're a victim of the same thing you tried to do—chase the hangers-on. Or did you get set up by a strong hand, waiting for just such a move?

I am not a big advocate of bluffing late. In this situation the first raiser, who is not strong, must decide to either carry out his bluff with a reraise or call and expose the fact that he was not particularly loaded. You DON'T bluff with a lousy pair this late when there are three or four opponents still alive. I adamantly disagree with that move.

However, if I had two pairs, I'd raise when I had the last move and would reraise the bumper unless he had a flush showing or a pair on board. But if that was the case, a good player with two pair would not raise a pair on board or a three flush showing—especially if the pair was higher than his highest pair or if no mates to the opposition's pair were on board. With two pairs, I'm content to get a cheap ticket to sixth street.

But fifth street is decision time. If it ain't good, I'm gone.

32

Fifth Street Analogies

When I made a video on seven-card stud, one of the things I harped on was the fact that fifth street was my biggest decision point in the hand. After that, the betting gets heavy, and if you reach sixth street still on the come, you'd better hope the opposition isn't sitting with a loaded gun.

I received a ton of letters from experienced poker players, especially those involved in the now-popular card rooms in California. Most of the notes zeroed in on the fact that the betting does heat up after fifth street, and a few logical drops if you're not strong at that point do ease the pressure on the bankroll.

Again, it goes back to reading the players and trying to pick up patterns they follow, based on the playing of their hands and the original outcome. Most poker players adopt a style and stick with it. I admit I do have to warn myself to break my patterns so as not to get typecast. Do you know how hard it is to fold with a four flush on fifth street, or trips, or two high pairs? But a good poker player who has a position edge and a read on an opponent's strengths and weaknesses must have the guts to toss in a decent hand when it's obvious there are two or three power hands eyeing the same pot.

You can read a player shooting for a boat or flush on fourth street if suddenly he starts banging in the chips early when he usually plays semitight until sixth or seventh street.

Suppose you've got your four cards to a king-high flush in spades on fifth street plus a king of hearts for a power pair.

You're already counting the up-faced spades when three hearts, including the ace, makes a raise. Each of you has two cards of the other's suit accounted for, but he has that ace and a raise to boot. You haven't had a hand for an hour, and now you're sitting on the brink with the four flush and kings, two cards to go, seemingly nothing from three other payers, but a glaringly possible ace-high flush from the raiser.

Do you call and pray you catch your flush, even though you may need the still unseen ace of spades? Do you raise to find out if he has his flush?

No on both counts. But I would raise if I had my flush, even if the ace was showing in his hand, and wait for his reaction. At least I'd be strong enough to probably get rid of the other players. With the four flush, I merely fold and stay glued to his hand to see if he had his flush or bluffed me out. Either way, I won't chase into sixth street. My decision to continue to sixth street has to have me sitting strong with a flush or at least having two pairs to counteract the raise by the possibly higher flush.

The aggressive players will disagree with this reasoning and say you can't win if you're not in at the end. Man, how I hate that stupid philosophy. Do they expect everyone to ride every hand to the end with less than good cards?

Incidentally, if I were sitting with that four flush and kings paired and the bet reached me with no calls, I surely would raise. The reason is twofold: Where is the competition? And let's see if we can chase the hangers-on. I do not raise with two pairs but would if I had trips. And if there were a raise, I'd reraise if my trips were higher than the highest card the raiser had on board.

33

Wrapping Up Fifth Street

Many years ago when I was getting my clock cleaned regularly at the tables in Vegas, I was of the opinion that I could win every hand, or at least the majority of them, because I knew how to play poker. I never dreamed of giving credit to the other players in the game. When I lost, I hated the guy who beat me out. I vowed to make him pay.

I believed this until some sharp old-timers pulled me aside and ripped my style to pieces:

I stayed too long.
I stayed till the end with weak cards.
I bumped too early.
I held grudges.
I had more tells than the rest of the table combined.
I rarely quit when I was ahead or when I was going bad.
I talked too much.
I was afraid to fold on middle streets (fourth or fifth)

It was uncanny how they read, picked apart, and zeroed right in on my play and backed it up by beating me.

I listened and learned, mostly how to pick up even the tiniest flinch in the face of another player. It took concentration and the desire to win. I wanted to stay in every hand, figuring I'd catch, but never, ever realized the enemy could also catch if he wasn't already loaded. I did not become a conservative player, but a varied one, setting up opponents by making moves contrary to two or three that I did several hands back. You've got to have the guts to quit when you're beat or when you think there is an excellent chance that you will be.

I am not afraid to raise, but the key is showing absolutely no sign when you make your move. In the casino, you cannot string out your bet—it must all be made with one singular move.

Suppose a player bets $10 and is raised $10 by another player. If I wish to raise it to $30, I must put the entire amount in at the same time. You cannot say "Your $20," slide in $20 and come back with "and I raise $10." You must make it in one move: "Raise $10 or "Make it $30." This is done so you won't sucker the next guy into starting to make a move before you announce your raise, thereby picking up his intentions.

I zeroed in on fifth street as my catalyst point. Sure, I get beat sometimes when a lesser hand holds up and I folded with the winner. But that's gambling and part of cutting losses. I play tight, strong, loose, cautious, and aggressive when I get that fifth card. If I'm loaded, I'll act as if I'm looking around for a potentially strong hand when actually I'm dying to get raised.

The next time in the same situation, my move will be different, but fifth street is decision time and this theory has cut my losses dramatically. I rarely get hammered by a power hand when I am sitting so-so. You don't have to adopt this point as your decision time, but kick around in your mind how many times you headed into sixth or seventh street with subpar hands. It gets expensive.

34

Sixth Street

If you reach sixth street, you've either got a competing hand, an excellent hand, or you're a fool who should be playing jacks in a sandbox.

As you progress through the world of poker you'll find that at sixth street, you're gonna be subjected to raises and moves to check your gut level. Occasionally you'll get a player riding a bluff with a four flush on board and nothing down. He may decide to go all the way with his bluff, and it can be expensive if you're sitting with a weak hand.

At this stage of the game you're gonna see almost everything each of your opponents has because all four of their cards are staring at you. It's snap city to get a line on a person going for a straight or flush, but now you gotta wonder if they have it or if they are just playing on the come.

Here is where the experience and guile of the pro or sophisticated gambler comes in. The novice or ego-driven player has a false sense of his skill. You might hear him say: "OK, Mac, let's see if you really are sitting there with that flush." And he bets the max.

Stop right here. I'm not saying you shouldn't bang in the chips to get the four-card flush to make a move by calling if he doesn't have it or reraising if he has. My point is that you should take it one step at a time, and the first priority should be to check out your own hand. If you're facing a possible straight or flush with trips, it is NOT necessary to challenge a better hand. You have only one card to go and don't yet have your boat.

Merely check to get a line on the potential power of the competition.

At sixth street, a large bet is not gonna chase a player who already has his flush or straight, so the move is not to build up the pot but to try and get a reaction or try a bluff. It's too late in the game to try to get a read, especially when the potential on board is higher than what you already have.

It is not a sin to check your trips, or lower flush, if you're staring at a power hand. You should raise for a purpose and not in situations where there is doubt that you are sitting in the top spot. I use raises:

1. to get out hangers-on at fourth and fifth streets when I am decent
2. to get a read on opponents on fourth and fifth streets
3. to make a point of possible early power on fourth or fifth street
4. to establish a power move when I am loaded on sixth street

Look at (4). I'll bang up the pot on sixth street if I've already made my full house, flush, or read the remaining players as being less than I am at this point.

I told you earlier that if you get this deep in the hand you'd better be strong because the players who are sitting pretty will definitely make you pay. You can be sure I am not on the come this late in the game unless I have a medium to large pair, four cards to a flush, and very sparse betting and raising in the early rounds.

For the 843rd time I suggest you concentrate on reading your opponents. Instead of trying to act like Good-Time Charlie, carrying on useless dialogue, looking around the casino, or running to the john when you're out of a hand, use the time to pick up info on your quarry.

One final note on your being on sixth street with two pairs, trips, a straight, or a flush when two players are banging each other: There is no need to stay in! If you feel your flush is no match for a player who has been banging the pot since third street and probably has caught his boat, don't be afraid to fold. Better to fold than be caught in the middle of multiple raises with only one card to go and another series of raises coming, especially if you've reached your max value.

Will you lose some pots you might have won? Of course, but this is a money management tool that is essential to survival. It takes guts to fold when you feel you're beat, whether by one opponent or when stuck between a couple of raisers.

35

Sixth Street Varieties

Before a lot of you poker diehards start having convulsions about my conservative approach to gambling, let's step back and review what I perceive gambling to be—a chance to make money at the game you are most proficient at.

It is easy to stay in every single hand of poker. You'll find players with heavy bankrolls who stay in every hand, raise at every opportunity, steal antes, and glom a lot of pots by raising the competition right out of the game. These people are not good players but merely try to overwhelm those playing short. In a big game, these bangers are eaten alive.

I play with these dorks every day. The temptation is to play his game and try to outlast him, but you will find yourself doing the same stupid things he does. My theory is to play a strong conservative game, sprinkle in raises at third and fourth streets, make your key decision at fifth street, and have the brains and guts to fold when it appears you are beat. Sure it hurts to fold a decent hand on fifth or sixth street when a sharp player uses a couple of raises and forces you out of the hand because his up cards appeared to be something they're not. When you watch the final declaration of cards on seventh street, you find you could have won the hand!

You can't let that bother you; you can't relive every decision that goes against you and recant how you got bought out. If you establish a powerful theory of playing poker in such a way that you can confuse your opponents as to your methods on each succeeding street, you'll win your share of hands and cut your losses to the bone.

When I reach sixth street, I have something to play with and am definitely not on the come for an open-ended straight or looking to boat two pair versus a very obvious set of trips.

Remember the word value and how it applies to poker. Sometimes a pot has been the object of checks all the way to sixth street where only three players are hanging on in a rather dull hand. You have a pair of queens that appears to hold up against two other players who are content to check their way to this point with at least a small pair. On sixth street you do not improve your queens and the other two appear to have caught at least a second pair. A max bet and a raise come to you.

There is no value in the pot. At least one of them apparently has caught something, and while your queens may be the obvious high single pair, the value of the pot and the pattern of betting indicates it ain't worth the call.

All the crap about not dropping when you have the board beat is baloney. Check your hand and look at the betting patterns and the value of the pot. You gotta weigh all the pluses and minuses. If it ain't worth the now increased wager, DROP.

It's called money management and it's a sharp move.

36

Wrapping Up Sixth Street

Just like you need two varying opinions to make an argument—
two to fall in love, two ways to skin a cat (I'm told), two people to
tango—it is also said that two theories could both be different,
yet neither wrong.

That is the message I am trying to convey to you about poker.
Sixth street is such a situation. There are theories that say if you
get this far, make the other guy pay for the right to see that other
card. While I agree with that thinking, I am of the opinion that I
ain't gonna blow my wad trying to get players out by betting
crazy one step from the final card.

Who is to say which theory is correct?

You know how I feel about a conservative approach and I
think it should be carried through to the end of the hand. If I get
this far, I'd better have something—but the other guy probably
does, too. You ain't gonna get him out this late in the game, so
my advice is to check, unless you're boated or have a high flush
which seems unchallenged, and see what seventh street brings.

Give the other players the benefit of being strong, too. This,
to me, is a cautious street. Knowing how to use the check, if
you've been aggressive throughout the hand, can put your
opponent back on his heels.

The check is a powerful tool on sixth street, because of the
check and raise possibility. Checking is not necessarily a
conservative move because when you are loaded and make a
max bet you may get a lot of calls or drops. But if you are loaded

and check, you may pick up a couple of raises, some additional stays by players on the fence, and the always open chance to come back with a reraise.

Gambling is 75 percent money management, and sixth street is a great place to use all your cunning and devious tactics.

37

Seventh Street

Remember the old saying "If you got it, flaunt it. If you don't got it, fake it." Showgirls in Vegas and other performers have been doing OK for many years with this philosophy. It obviously works for them. Of course the dorks these women set out to trap or con are guys like me, who away from a poker table could easily carry the label "fish."

At the table, and especially on seventh street, is where you do your flaunting. If you have a power hand, make them pay! When I get to this point with a hammer between my fingers, I'm raising, reraising, and giving the rest of the table good reason to think twice about stealing a pot.

DO NOT show your hand if you kick someone out because the element of doubt will be needed down the road in another hand.

If you reach seventh street loaded and have the bet, you can go for the max if you think the other players fear your hand and have been calling you the last few cards. Try to get the max for being strong. However, if you are strong and are against another player who is likely to raise or has raised you at sixth street, there is no reason not to check, look for a raise, and come back with a reraise. If you're boated or very strong, you feel pretty safe so you've got to play hardball on seventh street.

DO NOT show your cards if everyone drops. Or have I said that before?

If you reach this street, you should have something. But now you need to be able to read your hand in comparison to the

competition. Don't be afraid to check your trips if you smell a
straight or a flush. Don't give any indication that you're weak
with a check, but decide ahead of time exactly what you'll do at
this point. The betting sequence at seventh street is identical to
sixth as the up cards won't change. So the sharp players will
look for any tells at this point.

If you checked at sixth street with a small flush and had the
bet, go to that move again. Make them try to figure out if you
had your hand all along or were looking for a check or raise. If
you do not have to bet, look for telltale signs of reluctance on the
part of the bettor if he bet strong on sixth street. If he looks
around the table, hesitates, or does extra thinking, go after him.
Maybe he is leading you on, but I like to show aggressive moves
on seventh street as a message.

If you're sitting with a questionable two pairs or small trips,
seventh street is definitely not the place to bang in a raise. Try to
get to the finish as cheaply and as quickly as you can.

In this instance, DON'T fake it if you don't got it. Seventh
street is not for foolish moves. Strong hands will make you pay
dearly.

38

Wrapping Up Seventh Street

You don't need a long, drawn-out map of things to do at this point. Poker playing is done on the early streets. At this point:

If you're strong, make them pay dearly by any means possible.
If you're weak, drop or call only if you read the opponent to be a little shaky.
If you're decent but not powerful, just call. Your time for raises and reraises is when you're in fat city.
If you're undecided about your two raisers, you must drop. I know this hurts, but banging a brick wall with a flawed tool makes no sense.

Of these four situations, the last is hardest to do because you hate to toss in a hand that may end up the strongest in the game. But give your opponents the benefit that they too could be strong. You wanna cut your losses to the bone.

By the time you've reached seventh street, you'd better have a competing hand because now the raises and trickery begin. I truly believe that the earlier streets are more important as you jockey with the other players to try and get a read on their hands or make them confused over what you are holding. That is where the art of throwing in your hand, raising, checking, reading your opponents, and setting up your game plan comes in.

On seventh street you either have a great hand where you

make them pay, a fairly good hand where you use checks and calls to cut losses, or you read another player as being stronger than you and have the guts to toss in your hand.

What else is there to say about your play at this point? If you get reraised when you are strong, you have two choices: call or reraise. This is your decision, based on what you see. There ain't no set rules for me to put on paper for you to follow. If I am strong, I come right back with a reraise. But if I am sitting with trips, a low flush, or two high pairs, the move is just to call.

It always amazes me to see a player with two pairs banging heads with another player on seventh street in a series of bumps. There is no point. The ego is involved, and ego has nothing to do with poker or winning.

39

Flushes and Straights

You don't have to be a raving genius to realize that if you have a royal flush, straight flush, or four of a kind, you've got a good shot at winning. But how many of those hands have you had in the last couple of years? Not many, I can safely assume.

Next, we'd like to have a full house, and while they don't pop up all the time, when they do, you're in good shape. And don't tell me any war stories that every time you're loaded with a boat, somebody comes along and gets one higher. That's gambling, so if you can't stand the heat, get out of the kitchen.

I don't have to tell you how to handle your betting in these instances: Raise as often and as high as you can, and hang all that crap that you wanna keep everybody in to build up the pot. What nonsense, leaving yourself open to being outdrawn.

But the next set of hands is the flush and straight. I've already told you I don't chase straights and have to fall into one to get into that position. In every hand you'll see a possible straight developing because the opportunities are so prevalent. If you're paranoid about straights just check out how many 5s and 10s are used up. Without a 5 or 10, there is no way a straight can be completed. So I always keep a look out for these cards, based on the cards showing straight (whether high or low). Every low straight up to a 9 MUST have a 5 in it. Every high straight (6 through ace) MUST have a 10.

If a player has 8C, 9S, 7C, JS on deck, I know he needs a 10 if he is looking for a high straight and a 5 if he is going low. If he's still around with that mishmash on board, that's probably what he is looking for. Just watch his betting patterns. If he checks, he didn't catch. If he raises, he's going for—and has—his straight.

But I zero in on the playing of flushes. I am thinking flush every hand and even admit to calling on third street when two of my cards are power and suited. If fourth street is off suit, I drop. If I catch my third suit on fourth street, I'm checking for accountable cards of that suit from the rest of the table. I've got three suited in four cards and need two in the next three. If there are about five of my cards showing and I have three at fourth street, I'm gone. There are too many cards I can't see and I need two catches in the next three cards to get my flush. But if there are only two showing, along with my three of four cards, I'm in for another look for anything less than two raises on fourth street, which admittedly is rare.

Yeah, I think flush a lot and like my chances of getting a decent read on how many are played and how many are still unaccounted for.

But I rarely think straight, so they become almost nonexistent for me.

40

Synopsis of Stud

The next chapter takes a look at a game I play all the time: hi/lo stud. Naturally, it is a spin-off of the basic seven-card variety that is so popular in both the casino and the weekly home get-together.

You should realize by now exactly how I feel about poker. It is a great game to play and maybe the best of all casino games because it is based on your skill as opposed to that of the players at your table.

With the table limit rule in effect, you can cut your losses by buying in for lesser amounts than you're forced to use at the other table games. Your buy-in protects you. Just remember the minimum requirements. For a game of $1–$3 or $1–$5, you can buy in for $20, but I suggest $40 and no more. In the $5–$10 game, the rule is usually ten times the amount of the minimum; thus you may be required a $50 buy-in. That's OK, but to feel comfortable I'd suggest $100 and no more. If you buy in with $200 at a $5–$10 game and get stuck with a bettor who is banging every pot, you may have a hand where you're sitting on the fence (trip deuces), get stuck in a triple-raise situation, and wind up with too many chips in front of you, rather than being able to play all in. If you had $15, you'd invoke the all-in move, allowing you to remain in and be free of all future raises.

A large buy-in causes you to call too many raises with suspect hands, so get into the habit of restricting your buy-in to $100 in smaller-stake games. When you get to the $10–$20 game, you need $100, but my suggestion is $150 to $200, with the latter the absolute max. Don't think you gotta buy in with the family jewels.

Learn to read the players at your table, to judge the value of your hand, and to put that nonsense about laws of probability out of your head. Here are a few tips to abide by:

Stay in low games until you're a perfect player.
Don't take on any teams in the higher games just yet.
Restrict your buy-in.
Read other players.
Read the value of your hand.
Don't bet like a rock on third street, but vary your calls when you are semidecent.
Don't fall in love with straights.
Don't zero in on "getting" a player.
Leave the table if you've got an ante-stealer or constant raiser.
Leave the table if you're getting poor hands.
Concentrate on the betting patterns of players on the previous street.
Zero in on flushes.
Try to account for as many cards as possible of a suit that you need.
Make fifth street your point of decision.
Don't go to sixth street unless you've got at least a good hand.
Don't be chasing at sixth street.
Don't be afraid to raise on fourth street.
Don't be afraid to drop on fourth or fifth street in the face of two strong hands when you are only decent.
Don't get overly aggressive on sixth and seventh streets unless your hand is loaded.
Don't think bluffing is a big part of poker. It ain't!
Learn to use checks.
If you read that you're beat, even with a decent hand, you gotta throw it in. It's more important to cut losses and not get stuck in a raising situation.

If you're strong on seventh street, sock it in.
Don't show your cards.
Forget your ego! You can't and won't win every hand.

Will you listen to these suggestions? I dunno—but I'd settle for two and be thrilled if you followed at least six.

Next we go into hi/lo, but we'll come back to seven-card stud when we reach the money management section.

Hi/Lo

41

Hi/Lo Stud

This is the part of poker I enjoy explaining. It is a type of poker I play all the time, whether in house games or in the casino. In fact, I play this as compared to regular stud poker seven sessions to three. Immediately I hear the cries of those poker players who hate this version of the game. Their gripes are:

I don't wanna split my pot with anyone.
I hate the boredom of this game.
It throws off my thinking to go for a low hand.
The pots are too small.
There are too many rocks in these games.

All the above may be applicable, but it's all in how you look at the game.

My humble opinion is that I have two shots at a profit, and since I don't give a rat's tail how much I win (only how little I lose), it doesn't matter that there's no potential for gigantic pots in this game. The fact that you can win either a great, strong hand or a great, lousy hand has always drawn me to this table.

By now you probably know the object of the game: Half the pot goes to the highest hand and half the pot goes to the lowest or worst hand.

There are many variations of this game, but once you learn the basic ideas, the house rules can easily be picked up. The basic rules are:

1. It is played exactly like regular seven-card stud, starting with two cards down, one card up.
2. Low card bets first.
3. On fourth street, it reverts back to high hand betting first.
4. The last card dealt is face down.
5. Players complete betting on seventh street.
6. Rules vary, but players split the pot between the high hand and the low hand.

Nothing complicated about the basic approach, but let's go to (6) since there are variations in declaring your intention to go low or high.

In the house game version, which I like better, the move begins after the final bet on seventh street. All the players left in the hand must declare whether they are going low, high, or both. If you decide to go for both sides of the pot, you must win BOTH high and low. If you lose either side to another player, you forfeit your right to either the high or low pot. I'll explain this further, so just hold your britches.

At the completion of the betting, all remaining players grab a couple of coins or chips and put their hands under the table. When everyone is ready to declare, the players open one of their hands to show their intent:

no chips... going low
one chip... going high
two chips... going high and low, but must win both (You're not holding your britches. I'll explain this later.)

Of the players who declare low, the lousiest hand wins the low half. Of the players declaring high, the best five-card hand wins the high pot. If everyone goes low (or high) the whole pot goes to that hand's winner. Many times you'll see a player guess that everyone is going high, and he'll go low just to try and steal that portion of the pot. Again, we'll get into these situations a little later on.

Therein lies the basic idea of the game. I like it because it offers interesting opportunities to back in to a payoff. Most dyed-in-the-wool poker players hate it because they end up with a full house and have to give 50 percent of the pot to someone with zilch.

In the casinos, the hi/lo pot is NOT declared. At the end of betting on seventh street, you turn over your cards and the dealer declares winners and losers. Your hand speaks for itself. You can still win both ways but can also win just high or low.

Don't make your decision yet as to whether you like it or not. Read On!

42

House Rules in Casino Style

For some reason, the casinos have come up with variations of the house or private versions of hi/lo.

Besides the change in declaring whether you are going high or low, there is a number placed on how low your hand can be. The number is 8, and it's called hi/lo, qualifier 8. It means you cannot have a card higher than 8 to declare low. Suppose you have a nonsuited 2, 3, 5, 6, 9. You cannot go low because you're over the minimum of 8. If you have a nonsuited 2, 3, 5,, 6, 8, you can qualify for the low hand.

I vehemently disagree with this rule change. In house games, you can declare low with any hand, even a pair if you feel so inclined.

My friend Reid P. Layer is a great reader of players, as you should be. In house games where you declare your intention of going low or high after seventh street, Reid P. Layer takes stock of all the hands. Let's say he reads one as going for a flush and two others have three or four cards that indicate a straight or high pairs. He may take his hand of 4, 7, 9, J, Q, 4, K and declare low, though 4, 7, 9, J, Q is not usually a good low call. Reid reads the other players as going high and takes a shot at stealing a low. Many times this would hold up because he read the players correctly. But this is not allowed in the casinos because of the low 8 qualifying rule. I do not like that rule. It is too cut and dried.

In the house game you gotta win both ways if you declare you're going both ways.

Let's say you gave a hand of AC, 2C, 4C, 6C, 7C, 5D, AH. You declare both ways, with the five clubs being your high and AC, 2C, 4C, 5D, 6C being your nonflush, nonstraight, 6 low hand. You've got a great shot at both hands of high and low.

In the casino, you would have both these hands judged against the other players' hands, and you may win just the high, just the low, or maybe both. Cards tell. But in the house game, if you say you're going for both high and low, you'd better win both. Then you'd get both pots.

I like the house rule of declaring which way you're going and the opportunity to have no qualifier. And I agree with the house rule that if you declare both ways and only win one, you forfeit everything. Then the pot gets divided among the winning hands who declared high or low. If you declared high but saw you could have won low, you would NOT get that low pot in house games. You would in the casino.

As you can guess, I prefer the house game of having no qualifier, declaring your preference, and needing to win both sides if you declare both.

There is one more rule worth mentioning. In house games, a nonsuited 1, 2, 3, 4, 6 is a perfect low. In the casino, a perfect low is a nonsuited 1, 2, 3, 4, 5. Naturally, that hand also counts as a straight, giving the casino player a good shot at both high and low.

Yeah, I like 1, 2, 3, 4, 6 as the perfect low, still siding with the house rules. It requires more concentration and cleverness to manipulate the 1, 2, 3, 4, 6 than to just get both sides handed to you.

Finally, in the casino the highest straight is a nonsuited 10, J, Q, K, A. The next highest straight is a nonsuited 1, 2, 3, 4, 5. That means a straight of 9, 10, J, Q, K loses to 1, 2, 3, 4, 5. It's too much edge to give that ace. Again, I lean heavily toward the house game or private game where 2, 3, 4, 5, 6, and any other nonsuited five cards, beats 1, 2, 3, 4, 5.

Maybe I'm old-fashioned, but I vehemently disagree with all the changes the casinos put on this excellent game. But I play it anyway!

43

Keying the Game

In all my books and tapes on gambling I speak about "keying." This is especially true in my sports book where you zero in on a certain team or "key," betting over or under.

For instance, in baseball, the Cleveland Indians are such a powerful offensive machine that many of their games produce runs in double digits. For that reason, I key betting over. I look to bet over the number the *Sports Book* puts out on their games. Let's suppose Cleveland is playing Detroit and the over or under number is thirteen. I wanna bet over, but I won't challenge that high a bet. So I pass. I'll bet the game over ten and a half or eleven if there is a lousy pitcher on the mound for both teams, but otherwise it is a pass. You look to bet over and then adjust your thinking based on the pitchers listed for both teams and the base number.

In basketball, I key the New York Knicks under. I wanna bet them to be involved in low-scoring games because their present players—John Starks, Anthony Mason, Charles Oakley, etc.— ought to take out membership in a cement union. In other words, they toss too many "bricks" at the basket. When the line comes out, I look to bet under; but say the man drops the figure too low—for example, 179. I pass.

So understand that keying is determining a way to bet and either going that way or passing on the bet if the number is out of whack. But never swing over and bet the other side. Then the man has you making a bet contrary to what you predetermined to do. If you key over and the line is high thirteen or fourteen I do NOT switch to under. I pass.

In hi/lo, I key Low. I wanna go low and try to zero in on the players around the table who would be my competition. This doesn't mean I sit at a table, key low, get dealt trip queens, and toss them into the muck because I don't wanna bet high. This is different than sports betting, although you do set out keying on a side.

Everybody grows up playing poker looking for high hands, so psychologically we are always thinking power hands and automatically gear our behavior along those lines. Believe me, strong hi/lo players think low first and adjust if they are dealt possibilities toward the high. Then comes the art of checking the table to see where the competition may be heading.

In games with no qualifier, I find keying low to be beneficial when you have the opportunity of going low with anything.

The following chapters will take you through the streets of poker, just like we did with basic seven-card stud hands. You can make adjustments along the way, but keep this keying factor in the back of your mind.

I think my fascination with low came way back in high school when I made a stupid pass at the homecoming queen. It was probably off-color because I remember her words: "You're so low, you have to look up to look down." Ever since I've thought low, and it's worked! So maybe that stupid pass turned out to be a home run. Or is it touchdown?

44

Third Street

You don't have to be a college graduate to understand what to do in hi/lo when you're dealt your first three cards. It is much like regular seven-card stud except now you are also thinking low.

When I get that up card and two downs, I pray for three low cards (7 and under). Let's say I have a nonsuited 6, 5, 3. I am not even considering a straight, but my eyes scan the board to see how many other hands show a low up card. Yes, I stay. And yes, I call any and all raises with that great a start. In hi/lo you rarely see ante-stealers on the first three cards because players who can go either way must realize nobody is that strong this early and all low players will definitely stay.

If I'm dealt two lows and one high (4C, 3D, QH), I'm in for a call but not a raise. And I never raise on third street. There is plenty of time to get a read on the other players, even if I have trips, a high pair, or three suited low cards. I still settle for a call, mostly to avoid drawing attention to my hand.

Let's suppose you are dealt AD, 2D, 5D, with the ace up. You have a strong shot at both the flush and low. By calling, you give your opponents no read on you, but a raise alerts sharp players that you are going low. You're giving away a dangerous tell!

I throw away a hand with KS, QS, 5D, even though in seven-card stud I'd use a call to avoid letting the other players think I'm a rock. In hi/lo, there is no value in chasing a flush for half the pot. As stated, I will call 2D, 3D, 10H if there are no more than three other players showing a low card. But I will only call a single bet on third street with two small cards and fold with even one raise.

Just as in seven-card stud, third street keys your staying, but you need not worry about staying with middle-of-the-road hands to avoid appearing like a rock. You'll get ample staying hands.

Third street is cool city—don't make any waves. And don't chase raises with garbage.

45

Fourth Street

Now we get to see two up cards from our competition, and this helps in the game.

A player that stays in on third street with a deuce showing gets our attention because he smells of a low. But if that player gets a queen on fourth street, we read him high, or three of four cards low, and his betting decision will give us a read. He surely won't raise if he's going low, so he either calls or drops. And that should be your method of play with that hand. Three of four low is a call. If you end up with 50 percent low and high and no three-card flush, you are out of this hand and should read the opposition the same way.

I'll stay on fourth street with a power pair, four cards to a flush, four cards low, or three cards low, with no more than three opposing players who have two low cards up and no raises. A good hi/lo player should raise with four lows at this point, and if I've got three, I'm gone with that raise. With three lows, you need two of three catches for your strong low, and even then you are liable to end up with a 7 or 8 as low card with a 6 low banging you around.

Most hi/lo regulars key low, so if you see one of these heavyweights banging the pot, you'd better be strong to take him on.

Be smart at this point because raises are gonna come from players with strong high hands trying to find out where other high hands are, knowing the low players will stay in if they read them high.

If you have QD, 10C up with a match in the hole, you surely should shout out a raise if you see low cards on most other hands. These players have to read you as high and will naturally call. Players going high have to make a decision to call because they know you are high and a strong hand going low will surely bang you back, igniting a raising war. If you are sitting with a medium pair versus a raise from an obvious high player, get out because you're gonna be caught in the middle.

When you see a raise from an obvious high hand and you are strong low AD, 2D, 4C, 8H, come right back at him. You'll chase low players trying to hang on and high players on the fence. Don't let low players stick around when you are decent on fourth street. I'll stay on fourth street with:

four low (raise if you have this hand)
three low
high pair
three cards to a flush
four cards to a flush; bang in a raise
a two-card low should get out, even with a small bet to call

Don't chase low hands with two low cards, even if the whole board shows most players appearing to go high.

46

Reading Players

Take a break right here so I can rehash a big part of my theory on playing poker. Even in this hi/lo game, the trick is getting a read on the opposition. Strong hi/lo players have patterns, and they center around:

keying low
raising on fourth and fifth streets with strong low hands
raising early with high hands, inviting reraises from low players to get rid of other high players
bluffing on fourth and fifth streets with all low cards showing, even with high cards in the hole

A bluff in hi/lo can be easily pulled off when the bluffer has low cars showing. Players going low with three of four low or four of five low will many times bite on this bluff, especially if the bluffer is showing possible low and flush. A player with QC, 10H in the hole and AD, 2D, 4D on board has a rotten hand. But the other players staring at these three low diamonds are swayed as to his going low, high, or both and can be conned into dropping. I'd surely raise in such a spot, especially if nothing of power is showing around the table.

Here is where reading the player becomes so important. Is that player a constant user of this method or is he a tight player taking a normal chance to raise? If I'm against a player so obviously strong, I'll stay only if I have four cards low or four cards suited. Otherwise, I'll go for his bluff and fold.

If you're in a similar situation, don't be afraid to run your bluff. If it fails, let the other players know you will run a play like that. It'll keep them in when you are truly strong. Since a bluff usually only works once, or at best twice, a session, you won't go back to that move again anyway. But unless you are powerful either high or low, you gotta fold your tent and run when a raise comes from an obvious low or high pair on board.

Read those cards—that's where the answers are.

47

Wrapping Up Fourth Street

It's pretty much an easy chore to decide whether you stay or drop at this point. You could be sitting with 2C, 4D, 8H, QD and drop if two or more hands show two low up cards. You're not strong enough to stay. But if that 8H is a 5H, giving you three strong lows, then you can hang a call.

Don't chase a low past fourth street unless you have three hanging low. Don't chase! Since most hi/lo players think low first, it's the sharp person who can read the table on fourth street as to the possible direction the competition is taking.

Don't think I'm giving you a license to raise or stay with a lousy pair of fives because I ain't. The betting is positively gonna get heavy on sixth and seventh streets between high and low players, with some power moves by several low players sitting with perfect lows or even 6, 5, 3, 2, A.

But fourth street does give you the opportunity to shoot a raise when you have trips, two pairs, a high power pair, or a four-card flush. You're inviting a reraise from a strong low hand, but what you're looking for is a response from an obvious high hand, whether he merely calls, indicating he's not that strong, or bangs you back to let you know he's in for the full run. If he calls, you can become more aggressive on fifth street to see if he improved. Even in a hi/lo game, your moves on fourth street should be similar to seven-card stud, except you can become a little more aggressive at this point to check out a hand you perceive as a threat. His reaction gives you the read you're looking for.

The main thing to realize when you are shooting for the high side is that you don't chase forcibly with a rotten hand, even if you read all other players as shooting low.

Suppose you have 5H, 9H, 5D, JS, and are facing a raise from one of the other four hands, all showing two low cards up. You have no right to assume they are all going low and definitely no right to stay for a call. You fold your collection of garbage and observe the final stages of a game where you don't belong.

You'll steal maybe sixteen hands in a lifetime if you play poker five days a week, so don't play a chump hand like a chump.

48

Fifth Street

Just as in regular seven-card stud, this is decision time and you should finalize your moves. Obviously, you'll stay with:

 five low (7 or lower) and insert a raise
 four low cards
 trips
 two power high pairs
 flush and bang in a raise
 four-card flush

These hands are easy to decide. It's the ones on the fence that make it tough to choose whether to stick around or run.

One thing to keep in mind in hi/lo is the power of suggestion that three low cards give out. It gets everyone thinking you are strong low and allows you to slip in a raise with the main chance of reraise coming from players going high. You can be sure a lot of raising goes on in this game, on sixth and seventh streets and even here on fifth.

If you have a four-card low with 7 as your key, you'd better think twice about whether two other low hands with possible 6s are sitting stronger than you. Personally, I'd like to see you fold a four-card 7 low, rather than take on two potentially better hands. Remember, if they are betting into you with no fear of your 7 low—fold!

My theory of making a decision in regular seven-card stud on fifth street does not change here—if I am going high. Maintain the same level of consistency in hi/lo. Don't head into sixth street, into the teeth of sure-fire raises, with two small pairs or a four-card flush when your perceived competitor is banging in a raise. I'll call at that point, but won't change my tactic of not chasing into sixth street with less than a strong hand.

A poor poker player sees hi/lo as a chance to steal pots from the high side when other players appear to be going low. He stays with lesser hands into sixth street, not realizing the hands that appear low could be possible flushes or even low trips.

All I'm telling you to do is play your high hand as you would in regular seven-card stud. Not all Low hands are definitely going low, and you could be caught in an expensive raising war.

49

Wrapping Up Fifth Street

No need to beat the fifth street theory to death. You can see the same approach in regular poker. The difference here is you have to realize the value of your bet is reduced by 50 percent because of the split pot.

If you have a perfect low on fifth street, you gotta raise every single bet to the max because you have a guaranteed win on the low side. If you're in the casino, you've got a chance of also winning high because a perfect low is an unsuited 1, 2, 3, 4, 5 with a shot at the straight. Even if you get beat in the casino with your straight, you can win on your perfect low.

In the house game, if you have a perfect nonsuited 1 through 6 low and a straight and you call both ways, you stand to lose everything if that straight loses. Still you gotta raise every chance you get with a perfect low. In a house game, if I have a perfect low, I go both ways if I have a flush or full house as my high. A straight is not strong enough to go both ways, so I'll grab the definite payoff for the perfect low. Of course, I'll go with the straight if the competition shows no chance of a flush or straight.

On fifth street you should call all raises if you have a nonsuited 1, 2, 3, 4, and any other card. The only time I'll stray from this is if there are four other 5s or 6s used up, cutting my chances of a 6 or 5 low. A lot of raises by two or three other players showing low hands on fifth street leaves open the possibility they could already have 6 or 5 low. Then you gotta fold your 1, 2, 3, 4!

In the same vein, if you are flushed on fifth street, keep raising those bumping lows because you have a great shot at the high pot and you wanna get out all possible high competitors.

Just as in basic poker, I make my decision to go to sixth street only if I'm loaded or have a working 1, 2, 3, 4. If I do not have trips or better, I drop unless it's obvious the high hands are not powerful. A player obviously going high will raise on fifth street. If I only have four cards to a flush, I'll fold in the face of a high-hand raiser if I see four or more of my suit around the board.

Remember the word *value!* Don't chase pots unless you've got it on fifth street, either high or low, because you're only gonna get 50 percent of that total pot. But if you got it, don't wait. Bang up every bet for the max raise.

50

Sixth Street

If you wanna dance, you gotta pay the fiddler. If you wanna fly, you gotta sprout wings. If you wanna be a politician, you gotta know how to lie. And if you wanna win at poker, you gotta be smart.

Smart doesn't mean counting to forty by twos, or spelling mom backward, or even saying the ABCs to P without cheating. Smart means knowing your opponents' moves and being able to read hands. If you concentrate on each hand of poker and catch the betting patterns during the early rounds, by the time you get to sixth street you should have a handle on just how strong your chances of winning really are.

At this point you can see four up cards of the other players, giving you a decent idea what you're up against. Plus you have six of your seven cards, 83 percent of the hand is over, and the betting patterns up to this point should surely have given you an idea who is hot and who is not. You gotta be smart and analyze your chances of winning, as opposed to pulling back and cutting your losses by yielding to the hand that appears stronger than yours.

Sure, you could fold a winning hand when you misread the opposition, but that's poker. My theory is, and always will be, geared to a conservative approach.

At sixth street check your hand because to pass fifth street you must have had a decent shot and now you get to see everyone's fourth up card. Did you improve? Did the competition improve? Based on the previous betting pattern, you should know where your opposition is most formidable.

If you have the lead bet, check if you see the challenger obviously improved and you didn't. It's an ego thing if you think you MUST bet because you've been betting all along. A check puts the onus on the other players to make their move. If they've improved, they'll probably bang in a raise. If you doubt how strong you are, call. If you feel you're stronger, come back with your own raise. But you don't have to take the macho approach unless you're sitting with a perfect low or a full boat.

If there is a lot of calling up to this point, I love to raise on sixth street to avoid letting the callers get a cheap ride. Two power pairs or better key my raise.

It all comes down to being able to read your possibilities of victory with 83 percent of the hand completed. If you don't acquire this art, you'll never be able to compete successfully over the long run. If you read that you're beat on sixth street, you gotta have the guts to admit defeat and fold.

I love sixth street because to get here, you know I have something. So I'll get aggressive to test the challenges.

51

Wrapping Up Sixth Street

This chapter won't be long because once you zero in on a method of play that is comfortable for you, the same method should prevail.

But let me rehash something I said early in the book. Every hand of poker differs from all others because of the method of betting from the other players, size of the pot, raising action to that point, and the fall of the cards. You could end up with a flush in three consecutive games on sixth street yet have to vary your tactics to comply with what is going on in each individual game. Maybe in two of these instances you are fighting a higher flush and a full house, and in the third other high hands are raising and reraising. You end up losing money to the stronger hands and winning a pittance when your flush has no competition.

So telling you what to do when you have trips, straights, flushes, two pairs, or a strong bluffing challenge from a habitual raiser will not help you at crunch time. Unfortunately, I can't lay out 243,627 possible things that COULD happen during the course of a session. But I can make you aware of how to handle yourself in different situations.

Hi/lo gives you many options, but the most important is being able to read people's hands for an idea of which direction they are going.

For instance, a hand showing 8H, 9C, 4S, KC is leaning high, probably a four-card club flush, or at best, an 8-high low hand but only four cards to that flush or low. Sixth street gives you this chance to get a read. A hand with 2C, 4C, 6S, AC is a dynamite low, yet holds a strong possibility of a club flush. Naturally, that player is in betting fat city and has control. If you ain't super strong at this point, you ain't wrong to fold.

Sixth street is a place where I have something to get there, then make my decision to go all the way by reading the opponents' cards as opposed to my own hand and recalling the betting patterns of the most powerful up hand.

Read those cards! They speak volumes!

52

Seventh Street

Nothing happens with the dealing of that seventh card because it's down and doesn't give you any opportunity to reevaluate the competition. If you are strong on sixth street and have your flush or boat, this card can only hurt you by helping the other hands.

The same strategy that prevailed on sixth street again rears its head. If you are sitting low, naturally you're gonna raise the high bettor—if you perceive little or no competition from the other lows. If those lows call, you'll probably get a reraise from the strong high bettor. If you're low and get no raises from the other probable lows, keep right on reraising with the obvious high.

This is where a player in a subpar situation of 8 low or two pairs can get caught in a raising war, which is why I beg you to have your hand on fifth street.

In hi/lo you'll see 60 percent to 70 percent of the other hands are self-explanatory because four up cards give you a nice read. Use that asset. If you're still uncertain but have a decent hand (either high or low), call or make partial raises to cut the amount of your outlay.

Let's suppose you have the bet with a pair of jacks on the board, and a third one down. You have trips but are skeptical of a three-card flush that is pointing high and still around on seventh street. Let's say it's a $20–$40 hi/lo game with five players still in. You don't have to check because then you're leaving three raises open.

Bet $5. If the flush uses one of the raises, he makes it only

116

$25. Naturally, the strong low raises $40 and it comes back to you. You don't wanna fold, so you call the $60 plus eat up the last raise with a $5 bump. Instead of a potential outlay of $160, you hold it to $70 by being able to manipulate the amount of the raises.

If I am sitting with 6 low or a high hand of any type full house, I'm raising the roof from the instant I get it. But betting and raising the max on seventh street with a suspect hand has always puzzled me. Give the other players respect. Maybe they're stronger than you and are sitting in the weeds waiting for the opportunity to bang you back. The few extra dollars you try to extract from the opposition at this stage is definitely unimportant unless you're in luck city. A good player either has you beat or won't chase those sucker bets. You are wasting your bets because this late in the game the sharp players won't make foolish plays.

Learn how to check, read, and run. Or have I said that before?

53

Raising

You don't raise every time you perceive yourself as having the winning hand. In low-stakes games you'll find players using the maximum three raises as soon as sixth and seventh streets arrive and sometimes as early as fifth street. That's because they are trying to extract max returns when they finally get a betting chance. Sometimes they finally get a hand. Sometimes they chase players. Sometimes they get reraised and eventually get beat out.

You've got to get so powerful in your analysis of the other players that a raise becomes a purpose move.

I am a great, great, great fast-pitch softball pitcher. I throw curves, drops, and change-ups 80 percent of the time and paint that outside corner constantly. However, my fastball could be caught one-handed by a seventy-five-year-old nun who never saw a softball game in her life.

Yeah sure, it's faster than the lobbly-gob tosses of you high-arc, slow-pitch players who bat .864 in a league where .600 hitters are considered patsies. But opposed to fast-pitch hurlers who throw bullets, my fast ball is zippo. So I use it as a purpose pitch. I'll stick it under a hitter's chin or at his knees, low and tight. It doesn't bother me to go 2–0 or 3–0 with these inside so-called heaters. I have the control to steal two strikes with outside curves and eat the batter alive with a down-and-away 35 MPH change-up curve.

All this is set up by the "purpose pitches." There are still some of those inside fastballs that stay over the plate and are promptly shot into orbit by assassins wielding aluminum bats. Do I deck those bruisers with my fastball in the left ear? No, I let the air out of their tires when I find where they parked their car. But that's another story. My purpose pitch more often than not does its job.

In poker, the raise should be used as a purpose move. Let the other players figure out what it is. Don't fall into the pattern of raising only when you're in lock city. But also don't raise when you have diddly-squat. That's only throwing money away. The next chapter goes into bluffing.

A raise is a dangerous tool that can be used to slow down a habitual banger and also to send a message. Don't overuse it because then it loses its purpose.

I've been pitching for more than thirty-three years and from day one I heard the catcalls: "His fastball couldn't break a pane of glass!" Maybe not, but it doesn't have to—it's only a purpose pitch to get a rise (or is it raise?) out of those hitting demons. Thirty years from now, they still won't know the reason for a purpose pitch.

I want you to use the same strategy with your raise. Your purpose? To make your opponents think.

Did I use the word *purpose* enough to get your attention?

54

Bluffing

I have absolutely no idea why the term *bluffing* is always associated with poker. It's like the way the word *jerk* is always associated with men. Well, maybe that's not a bad description because I gotta admit, we do have a knack for making jerks of ourselves. But that's another story.

I've been gambling since politicians were honest and for years words such as *bluffing, con, cheat,* and *double-dealer* have been associated with poker players. Yet these terms could also be associated with a guy trying to explain to his wife why he got home at five A.M. from a meeting with his accountant and why he had lipstick stains from his cuffs to his left ear. This guy is pulling out all the stops trying to bluff his way out of it, just as he has been doing for eleven years.

But in poker you really don't get that many opportunities to bluff. It is an overused expression and not necessarily one of a good player's primary approaches.

If I can set up my opposition for one bluff per night, I'm doing quite well. When you get into playing poker seriously, the people staring back at you from that card table are not exactly Dopey, Sneezy, Sleepy, and Doc. In reality, they are unpaid assassins who are cunning, wily, sharp, attentive, merciless, heartless, and ice cold. They are suspicious of some guy working on his third week of hay fever who reaches for his handkerchief in an awkward manner. Six sets of eyes wonder if he's banging out a signal to a friendly team member.

So don't go thinking you have to be a champion bluffer in

order to be a good poker player. Sure, you gotta throw off the competition by changing tactics, but not every move should be contrived to be a bluff. A good poker player makes moves to confuse the other players, and you must determine exactly what his purposes are. Setting up a key bluff hand takes many, many moves used at just the right time, but bluffing is a term that is worn out and blown out of proportion.

The best bluffers are those guys who tell their stories to the Queen of the Household and can still con her into letting them out again. Now those guys really know how to bluff.

Think about this message then reevaluate your idea that bluffing is a big part of poker. It's a part, but NOT a big one.

(I am guilty of bluffing about a piece of info I gave you in the beginning of the chapter. When I said, "I've been gambling since politicians were honest," you knew that statement was a lie. There never was a time like that.)

55

Wrapping Up Seventh Street

You've come this far in the hand, so obviously you have something. Now how do you play it?

Again for the 3,734th time: You check out your hand as compared to the four up cards of the players remaining in the game. Which of them was raising and how you perceive each in relation to your hand is the key. You do not stay if you're in doubt, you're not strong, and there is a bet and raise in front of you.

I hope you're not like my friend Juan Morshott, who is sitting with 10s and 8s and must decide if he wants to see that initial bet and raise. Juan Morshott will sigh, toss in his call, and moan, "What the heck is one more shot!" It's a stupid move on his part and just because he has contributed this far, he doesn't have to toss good money away.

I'm not gonna give you 430 examples of what the bettor has up or what the raiser has on board. The bottom line is that this late in the game both these hands see fit to bang in a bet. If either of them was suspect, the right move would be a check to test the water. If a player is stronger, he is gonna call anyway, or maybe even raise. You lead with a bet on seventh street when you're loaded so you make them pay to see your hand. The dope that can't grasp this philosophy is gonna get eaten alive going for just one more shot.

Obviously you NEVER show your cards when you drop because somebody is surely gonna get a read on how you played certain hands. You only show your cards when you wanna let them know you stayed with junk, were on the come, or dropped with trips to send out a message. This gives your playmates something to think about.

Seventh street is very much like sixth because you don't get to see that last downer. If it didn't help you, it still might have made a difference in two or three other hands and could become expensive. Personally, when I get to seventh street I'm more interested in cutting potential losses rather than squeezing out a few extra chips. If I'm loaded for bear, I'm gonna raise the roof. But on trips or lower, I'm content to merely glom that pile of chips.

Naturally, in most games when it comes to the last two players, there is an unlimited number of raises. That rule makes for good stories and high-tension made-for-TV movies, but who's to say that other cat ain't holding four little ladies? Will it really make that much of a difference in your life to get into an endless raising situation? To keep reraising when neither player will give in is a useless exercise. But then, I'm very, very conservative. I wish some of you would think along these lines.

56

Community Card

In hi/lo games you've got a great chance of using the entire deck if everyone is staying because you can go high or low. Many times that leads to all the cards being used, resulting in the use of a community card.

Let's say six people are still in on seventh street, but there are only four cards left, one of which has to be buried. The dealer will then announce to all the players that the next card is community, which means it is dealt face up and is used by every player.

I absolutely love this card because then I get to see five of each of my opponents' cards. If I don't have anything, I fold. But if I'm going low and think two other players are low, it gives me a great read. Look at some of the options that could turn up:

Card is a 4 and matches a player's 4, hurting his low.
Card is a 3C in a hand where player shows a 3D.
Card is a JS in a hand with three lows showing.
Card is a 7 and a player has queens paired, a jack, and an ace.
Card is a 10H in a hand with a pair of 8s showing, plus a 9 and another 10.

In each of these examples, I can now get a truer read as to whether those hands were helped or hurt by the community card. I already know what it did to my hand, and if it hurt it or didn't improve it, I'll fold and not care what it does to the others. But if I stay in, I get a bird's-eye view of how it affects the other players. Sure, they have the same opportunities, but the world is full of people who can't see the forest for the trees.

Sounds corny, but I want every teensy-weensy little edge I can get. Seeing that fifth up card is an edge.

It's like getting the first six digits of Anna Nicole Smith's private phone number. I play all the combinations, hit pay dirt, call the number, and a guy answers the phone. Well, you can't win every poker hand either, even with a leg up on seeing 72 percent of your opponents' cards.

57

Wrapping It Up

I love hi/lo, but I've already told you that. I play it all the time, but you already know that. I think you have a great chance to cut losses with this game, but that's already been said. So you're bored by these three facts already because you remember hearing them before.

Well, if you remember these little facts, why can't I get you to remember some of the things I told you about poker that will cut your losses and put you in a position to pick up a few bucks?

My style of poker and hi/lo is conservative but effective, and it points you toward a game that should be more popular than it is. The biggest reason I get from players who won't get into hi/lo is that they don't like to split that pot. If eight players are in a regular game, your chance of winning the whole pot is one in eight, or 12.5 percent. With eight players involved in a hi/lo game, there are two pots, so you have a one in four chance, or 25 percent, of picking up a return.

Since I believe cutting losses is more important than going for the kill, I am probably in the minority.

If you do give hi/lo a shot, try the tactics of getting a read on the other players' hands and counting the number of low cards that get used up to fourth and fifth streets. Try to get involved in a no-qualifier game because that mandatory 8 low takes away a lot of maneuvering from your game.

Do I like this game? That's obvious. Play it sometime. I think you'll like it, too.

Texas Hold 'Em

58

Texas Hold 'Em

In the beginning of the book I told you my messages on poker are geared to intermediate players and I assume you already know how to play seven-card stud. Since hi/lo is merely a spin-off of seven-card stud, we went right through the theories of that game.

Next we slide into a game that has been around for a while but is still foreign to the average poker player. It is called Texas Hold 'Em, and it is as popular now in Las Vegas, California, and Atlantic City card rooms as when poker first hit the tables many moons ago.

Since many of you have never played it, I will go back to square one in explaining it. You experienced players just bear with the basic explanation.

This game is popular because a lot of betting, raising, bluffing, and high pots are prevalent. You'll find it is a simple game to understand, but as with all gambling endeavors, the key to success comes in how you actually bet the game. In gambling, money management is, and always will be, king. I strongly urge you to play this game, but first a few comments about it.

I'm sure you'll like it, and I want you to play it. But as mentioned earlier, there is a lot of raising, position betting, and ante-stealing by sharp players who make a living grabbing antes and small pots with excessive and constant betting. They come loaded with high bankrolls, wait until they are in advantageous positions, and go after the rocks and conservative players who hesitate to test the validity of these big bangers.

In a nutshell, Texas Hold 'Em is a great game, a position game, and a game you'll go back to again and again. But you gotta have a decent stake and you gotta stand up to these phony raisers!

59

The Game

The game is played with a house dealer who is there strictly for the purpose of dealing. He has no monetary interest in the game and gets no cards. The house usually extracts 5 percent from the pot with a max placed on the higher-stake games.

There could be anywhere from three to ten players involved in the game. Everyone has a chance to be the so-called "designated dealer," which means that particular person is the last to make a betting decision, putting him in a great position. Since it is such a great spot, the house dealer has a puck or button that is passed to each succeeding player, thereby allowing a different player to be designated dealer each hand. As we go along, you'll see the power that goes with being DD or one of the two players to the DD's right. Those three hands bet last and many strong Texas Hold 'Em players really make the most of those strong betting spots.

But let's get to the game itself. The previous hand is completed and the HD moves the button in front of the next DD. Let's suppose we're in a $5–$10 game. The blinds, the two players to the DD's left, immediately place their respective bets. The term blind merely means you are betting on the blind, before you see your cards. The blind to the immediate left of the DD puts up $5 and the other blind puts up $10, which in effect is a raise.

No other player has to put up any ante, so the pot already has $15. The blinds MUST bet, but since you are not a blind, you don't have to ante until your turn based on the movement of the button. This way everyone in turn becomes blind number one, who, for example bets $5, and blind number two, who bets $10 then doesn't need to worry about antes until he is one or two seats to the left of the DD.

There are many players who jockey for position based on that button and leave before they get the shot at being a blind. The cheapskates who jump in and out of hands are soon caught so put that idea of trying to beat the ante out of your head.

OK, the blinds make their bets and each player is dealt two cards he can look at. DON'T show them to anyone! There are also five cards placed face down on the board, which the HD will eventually turn over.

The players examine their hands and the betting begins, starting with the third person from the left of the DD because the two blinds have already made their bets. Blind number one technically bet $5 and blind number two raised it to $10. The third player then makes his decision to stay or drop.

Got it so far?

60

Beginning

If the third player intends to stay, he puts $10 into the pot. If he decides to drop, he tosses his cards face down to the dealer. Actually he got to see two cards for free. (The next chapter goes over the strategy for staying or dropping.) The game continues as each player in turn either calls or drops after checking his initial two cards.

The betting amounts of the blinds are based on the limits of that particular game. We're talking $5–$10 right now, but it could be $1–$3, $2–$4, $3–$6, or much higher spread amounts like $50–$100. The bets made by the blinds are mandatory, then each player in turn makes the decision to call, drop, or raise. There is a strong edge for the players late in the bet because they have the opportunity to exercise their advantageous position—to raise and kick out the hangers-on.

Everyone benefits as the late bettor because of the movement of that button after each hand, and since the DD changes, each player eventually will be in those good positions. That's why this game leans so strongly to position play, and good players take advantage of the times they are sitting close to the DD's right. Naturally the DD has the best shot of all as he has the hammer as last bettor.

My suggestion, if you are sitting close to the blinds and have a decent starting hand, is to call the initial bets of the blinds. Don't chase if you ain't got the starting cards. You'll spend the whole hand chasing those who do have decent cards.

Before we go deeper into the game, I'm gonna list the hands and the rank of power they have. It's your decision whether to stay or drop but at least you'll have an idea how good or bad you're sitting.

61

Rankings

This is a list, in order, of the strongest hands you will be dealt. The opinions of Texas Hold 'Em players on such hands as 8, 8 versus K, 9 suited differ as you go deeper into the game. Which do you think is stronger? Some players say 8, 8 is better, others lean toward the K, 9. It is so close no one is wrong.

The following are my opinions and surely will draw negative comments from many quarters. (Note: (s) indicates suited.)

1. A, A	6. A, Q (s)	11. A, 10 (s)	16. J, 10 (s)
2. K, K	7. A, J (s)	12. K, J (s)	17. A, J
3. A, K (s)	8. K, Q (s)	13. K, Q	18. K, 10 (s)
4. A, K	9. A, Q	14. Q, J (s)	19. K, J
5. Q, Q	10. J, J	15. 10, 10	20. Q, J

Those are the strongest two-card hands you'll draw and with them you'll stay every time. The reasons are obvious. For example, A, K (s) is stronger than a pair of queens because an ace or king on board will immediately jump you over those queens even though you already have your pair. If you don't improve, you have the option of folding.

Let's go to the next twenty hands that are a step lower than the top ones:

21. 9, 9	26. A, 8 (s)	31. K, 10	36. Q, 8 (s)
22. 10, 9 (s)	27. K, 9 (s)	32. Q, 10	37. J, 8 (s)
23. Q, 10 (s)	28. Q, 9 (s)	33. J, 10	38. 10, 8 (s)

| 24. A, 10 | 29. J, 9 (s) | 34. 7, 7 | 39. 5, 5 |
| 25. A, 9 (s) | 30. 8, 8 | 35. 6, 6 | 40. 4, 4 |

Notice that you are starting to get watered down hands and if you feel obliged to fold for (37), J, 8 suited, don't feel bad.

Here are a couple more, but you're on your own from here on out. There's nothing written in stone that you should even call with these.

| 41. 3, 3 | 43. K, 9 | 45. J, 7 (s) | 47. K, 8 | 49. J, 9 |
| 42. 2, 2 | 44. Q, 9 | 46. Q, 8 | 48. K, 7 | 50. 9, 8 (s) |

That's enough because now you're just grasping for straws. I am NOT telling you to stay with every one of these combinations. I am listing them for rankings purposes only.

Suppose you're sitting under the gun or even two or three seats to the left of the DD and get dealt Q, 9 nonsuited. You could check but it's a certainty someone after you is gonna raise. Get out of there. Even if you have to see only a $4 bet in a $2–$4 game and you are early in the seating, my advice is to fold. You cannot win every hand in poker, so wait until you have some decent cards before you get in the hand.

In a game, you won't remember all the ranking so go back to the first twenty to get a grasp, then put them in the order you feel they belong. But the Top fifteen stay!

62

Terms

For those not familiar with some of the terms, let's go over a few and how they apply to the game.

HOUSE DEALER: Runs the game for house and handles all money transactions; has no financial interest in the outcome.

DESIGNATED DEALER: Each player gets a turn as dealer.

BUTTON: Marker to show who is DD for a particular hand.

BLINDS: The two seats to the left of DD who make their bets before hand is dealt.

FLOP: HD gives two cards to each player and places five cards face down on table. After first round of betting by players on their first two cards, dealer turns over three cards at once, called the flop, and then another round of betting starts.

NUTS: When you have a hand that is a lock or cannot be beat. When you learn to read cards on the table, you'll know when you have nuts. Until then, you're nuts if you merely guess!

POSITION PLAYING: Hold 'Em is a game where being DD or the last two players to bet gives you a big edge over the other players. Many sharks bet only when they are in these strong positions.

BACK DOOR FLUSH: If you are going for a straight or

trips and end up with the last two cards giving you a flush, it is called backdoor flush.

SUITED: Two or more cards of same suit.

THE TURN: After the flop, the fourth card or fourth street is referred to as turn.

ON THE COME: Aggressive form of gambling, where you are betting you'll improve your hand; a form of bluffing.

RIVER CARD: Last card of the flop or hand to be turned.

Learning these things ain't gonna make you a perfect player but will give you an idea of the terms used. It's still gonna come down to your reading the cards on board, analyzing your hand with these cards, cutting losses, and managing your money. That's gambling and it'll never change!

63

Quick Review

Let's bring you beginners right up to speed as to what this game is all about. Then we'll touch on how to attack it.

1. Hold 'Em has different levels of betting ($1–$3, $2–$4, $3–$6, $5–$10, $10–$20, $20–$40 and so on. Pick the limit that best suits your bankroll and buy in for an amount approximately twenty times the amount of limit (example: $100 for $3–6 game).
2. Most games are table stakes, so you are allowed to bet up to the total amount of chips you have at the table. You cannot buy more chips until that hand is completed, but you are in that pot for the amount you can cover.
3. HD moves button, allowing each player to be the DD.
4. Blinds place their wagers and HD gives each player two cards.
5. Players examine their cards and first player to the left of the second blind either calls, folds or raises.
6. Each succeeding player around the table does likewise.
7. HD had placed five cards face down on the table. Now he turns over first three, the flop, and another round of betting begins, starting with the first blind.
8. When that betting sequence is completed, HD turns over fourth card, the turn card, and another series of bets is made, starting with the first blind.

9. When betting is completed, HD turns over last card and last round of betting begins with the first blind. Last card is the river card.
10. At completion of betting, players show their hands, and HD pushes winnings to the high hand.

Players may use combination of five cards which could be one or two cards from their own hand and balance from the board. Let's suppose there are five suited cards on board for a flush. Everyone could use these five cards and there would be a tie. In the event the flop is, for example, As, Ks, Js, 5s, and 2s for a flush, someone might have a Qs in his hand and that person would win. This is the art of reading the cards.

If you are the one with the Qs, naturally you'd be betting heavy because there is nothing that could beat you without a pair on board since no one could have a full house. This is a lock! A bad reader might have the 10s and be betting crazy, not realizing the queen is still unaccounted for.

But that is the game of Texas Hold 'Em. It's very simple to understand, but now comes the tough part... reading the possibilities.

64

Reading the Cards

OK, you know what the idea of Texas Hold 'Em is. Now we reach the tough part to explain: reading the cards you can see on board.

Slip back to the chapter I gave you on deciding which cards to stay with. Some strong players stay with 9, 8 suited but I'm gone unless I'm sitting way deep in position and have only to call the blind. For that small call, I get to see the flop.

If two of those cards give me a four flush, I'll consider going for fourth street, depending on the amount of the bets leading up to my call. Don't forget, other players could have also gotten four suited and probably higher than my 9, 8. But basically I won't stay in a hand unless my first two cards give me a decent shot.

Then comes the flop and you now have five of the seven cards you're gonna get so you have a strong read on where you are headed. At this point you zero in on your possibilities and those of your opponents. In the previous chapter, the example given with that flush eliminated any possible chance of a full house. For a boat to rear its head, there must be at least one pair on board, so if you're sitting with a flush, you know a full house can't beat you if no pair shows. Same is true if you have a straight and only two of a suit showing. No one can have a flush, so you need only sweat out a higher straight.

Reading your hand after the flop is the first line of play, so analyze your chances of improving. I dislike giving you odds of such and such a thing happening because they change according to the next card dealt and the power of the hands you can't see. So I ain't gonna give you the odds of winning a hand when you go in with a pair and the flop gives you trips. Look at the other cards!

You're dealt 10C, 10H and call the first bet. The flop shows 10S, JS, 5S. You have trips but face three spades. There are six other players left in the hand and two of them bang in raises before it gets to you. No one could have a boat or straight so only trip jacks, trip 5s, or a flush is causing the raise.

Without trips I fold my 10s, but sitting in a deep position I'll call with my trips since I have two more shots for my boat. If I was on fourth street in this position and a 5C was the turn card, I'd be gone. I'd fear both the full house and the flush, so I fold with trip 10s. That's hard to do but it's fairly obvious you're up against at least two strong hands.

Go back to the call I made after the turn card. Suppose a pair shows with the 5 or jack. This chases me, along with another spade. Let's say a 9D shows and still two raises surface before it comes to me. I've got to respect those three spades, the raises, and now a possible straight with 9, 10, J. Many players stay with a K, Q, so another possible strong hand may have materialized. Reluctantly but definitely, I fold. This could be an expensive hand and the opposition may already have a flush or straight. I'm still on the come.

I ain't gonna give you six hundred possible hands, but you gotta learn to read those cards on the flop and how their possibilities relate to your hand. Also give credence to the raisers who start banging away after the flop when there are two suited cards or a pair on board.

Getting the drift?

65

Reading the Flop

Once you decide to call with your first two cards, the flop will be the determining factor as to whether you fold or continue to play. If you don't improve, get out. If you do improve, you'll stay for the turn card. The last possibility is a fair flop whereby you have an average hand and must decide to stay or fold based on what your opponents could have.

If you are under the gun with a fair hand—10D, 10C, and a flop of QD, KC, 2C—you're in trouble and can only check. You're fighting possible queens, kings, and even a four-card potential club flush. A raise sends me packing. With my initial 10s, I'd rather see all cards lower than 10 because jacks or higher leave open the possibilities of higher pairs. Don't chase those 10s. The flop didn't help you but probably did help the other hands.

Suppose you stay with QC, JC, and the flop shows AS, KH, JS. You now have a pair of jacks, but the king and ace have probably helped someone else to a higher pair. A 10 would give you a straight but leave open the possibility of a tie with someone else for an ace-high straight and a diminished split pot. Again, a raise will send me out of the game, especially with two other calls.

In this instance, higher pairs and even a four-card flush are staring me in the face. My jacks lose value quickly and I fold.

One more example to give you an idea of reading cards is when you are dealt AD, QD, and the flop shows JD, 8D, 8S. Regardless of where I'm sitting this is worth a raise to get out the hangers-on and also to give a message that you have something strong: either four-card flush, trips, two pairs, or even a full house. I doubt you'll receive a reraise unless trip 8s or a hidden pair of aces, kings, or queens takes a shot at you. But I would initiate the first raise to send a message and to draw out where the competition is. I would not reraise on fifth street but wait for the turn card. If I catch my flush, the raise is a definite. But unless I pair the jack, queen, or ace, I check or call the bettor. If the previous raiser again bangs in a bump, I head for the hills with a fold.

Get to respect the possibilities when there is a pair on board and you have not yet reached your max, in this case, the flush.

Let's suppose that after the turn, the board shows JD, 8D, 8S, 5H. That still leaves a bunch of possibilities to hasten my exit. No flush is possible but a full house, open straight, and four-card flush is still there, plus two pairs or trips. That's a lot of possibilities. You MUST fold. All it takes is reading the possibilities properly.

66

Practice

If you're new to this game, before you head to the tables, I want you to go through several practice sessions. This is done by dealing out hundreds of hands but looking only at your own first two cards, even though you deal out eight more two-card hands face down.

For practice only, each player will only flat bet, with no raising and everyone stays in until the end. Deal, turn the flop and you gauge your hand based on the flop, giving you five cards to calculate. Then go to fourth street and finally the last card is exposed.

The purpose is to see if you can read all the times that you have a lock, a good hand, a fair hand, or no chance at all. It is strictly to get you attuned to reading where you stand. Naturally, you can't read betting patterns because everyone stays in, but at least you'll see how easy it is to misread your chances. Eventually you'll see your mistakes and then get to ascertain the possibilities that the other hands possess, even though you may think you're sitting strong. You've got to learn how to instantly recognize all possible combinations to avoid staying with hands when you are buried.

For example, you're dealt KC, QC, and the flop shows AS, 5C, 5S. You are not in good shape because of the possibilities of the other players:

four 5s
full house, 5s over aces

full house, aces over 5s
trip 5s
two pairs, aces over 5s
two pairs, kings, queens, jacks, 10s, 9s, 8s, 7s, or 6s over 5s
two pairs, 5s over 4s, 3s or 2s
four spades, ace, king, queen, 5

You thought you had a decent hand with three clubs, pair of 5s or two high cards. Yet there are seventeen examples of hands that have you in trouble and the first couple are absolutely devastating. Yet you've gotta be able to read these possible hands as soon as they appear on the flop. That is the reason I want you to practice with your two cards and the flop coupled with the possible hands of all the other players.

It'll take some time to get acclimated to this card recognition, but it's a big step in being a good player.

67

Positive Betting

This chapter belongs in the money management section but I just wanna touch on it, while the previous chapter is fresh in your mind.

Let's say you become an expert at reading every combination that is available as soon as you see the flop. In fact I'll pop a few out for you right now. Grab a pencil and write out every possible combination that could beat your hand, which is a power-packed AH, QH suited—listed (6) in the chapter on rankings.

You feel comfortable until you see the flop. Now write down all the possible hands that could dim your initial joy:

1. AC, KC, KD
2. JC, JS, 10S
3. KD, QD, 5D
4. 8C, 8H, 8S.
5. 4C, 7C, 8C
6. AD, KD, 4D
7. 7H, 7S, KS

You're starting off with a strong suited AH, QH and in some cases have improved your status. But do you see the possible combos that you're up against, especially in a game with seven, eight, or nine players? Even after you zero in on all the possibilities, you gotta worry about how good a position you're in.

Naturally, if you're under the gun, you check or call the

blind. Raising this early in the hand leaves you open for a deluge of raises from players who may have improved their hands with the flop and you could get into an expensive hand. If there is a raise early, especially with flop hands (2), (3), (4) or (5), I'd call and not take on those potential powerhouses. Number (6) is also on the brink, particularly with a possible or Flush on the come.

Be sure you don't get into the habit of betting strong in the early positions because you are definitely prey for the tigers in the later positions. If you have a dynamite hand early, you can still wait for the turn card, then bet and reraise any bump that should come from the deep players, especially if there is no early raising.

Position betting is crucial in Texas Hold 'Em. Don't get aggressive in the early seats. If you are loaded after the flop and are seated deep, definitely shoot in a raise to get rid of the hangers-on. Don't let anyone stay around to outdraw you! You're sitting in fat city when you have a good hand and are in one of the last two betting seats. Take advantage of position.

68

Turn Card

There's no system here but let's say six to eight players are still in the game. You're gonna see a bevy of raises and reraises from:

bluffers
strong hands
medium to decent hands looking to chase hangers-on
heavy bettors looking to scare the rocks
position players who use that seat to exploit their power

Texas Hold 'Em is popular because of the excess betting and large pots. In Vegas it is more popular than regular poker and even the top tournaments draw big entries. The betting accelerated late in the hand makes the game so attractive. If you're sitting under the gun or close to the early seats, you'd better have a good hand to be able to sustain the sure-to-come raising from the deep position players in the late rounds. If you practiced reading the table with your two cards and the flop, then calculated the possible combinations that could occur, I'm sure you're surprised to see how often you're in trouble. Well, the turn card now has four cards showing, multiplying the possible combinations you are fighting.

Again, I want you to take a little time to analyze combinations you're up against at various points in the game.

You're sitting with a power pair of QS, QH, and the four up cards are JS, JC, 9C, 9S. You have queens over jacks and 9S and are looking for the boat. There are six players still in the game.

147

You ain't got diddly-squat, even though your pair of queens gives you the highest pair. That river card still to be turned over better be a queen. If it is a jack or 9 you still could have the highest boat because of your queens, but of the thirteen cards that could show up, you need a 9, jack, or queen to be competitive. That leaves ten cards that have you sitting with two pairs: ace, king, 10, 8, 7, 6, 5, 4, 3, or 2. That ain't such good odds.

If someone is sitting with two clubs or two spades, they are open for a flush. You also have the strong possibility that one, two, or three hands sitting with a 9 or jack already have a full house. Or a pair of aces or kings leaves other players way over your open three pairs.

The turn card gives you a look at a lot of combinations and you gotta be able to pick up the possible cards that could bury you. If I am early in the play and see two raises deep or even one raise from the latter position, I'm out of there. Suppose I am deep in the play and there are no raises early. I will not raise, even if I'm the DD because my hand is not that strong and there's probably someone waiting to jump back with a reraise.

The art of reading cards, watching for sandbagging (looking for someone to raise), and playing cat and mouse is all part of this game.

With four cards showing, it's unlikely you'll see a bluff with two pairs on board, so when the bets are free of raises all around the table, you gotta feel somebody has a 9 or jack and is waiting to bang back. Fourth street, or the turn card, shows too many possibilities for someone to try and steal a pot. If I have a full house at this point I'm gonna raise to the limit to get out as much competition as possible. But bet only if you have the boat and not on the come. On fourth street you're gonna see raises. Be sure you're strong before staying in.

69

Theories

I'm a very conservative player and gamble for two reasons: Money and action.

There is not a day that goes by—and that means 365 days a year, Christmas, Easter, and every other conceivable holiday—that I don't crave, want, or need action. The worst days of the year are the Monday and Wednesday surrounding the baseball All-Star Game when there are no contests. But on those days, poker and the racetrack do not take a holiday, so I have my "fix."

If I bet crazy, I couldn't last and no pro is really considered a big banger. That is usually reserved for the weekend or vacation player taking a shot. Most pros bet cautiously and protect their bankrolls because it is the only thing protecting them from, ugh, having to get a job! I bring the theory of being conservative to Hold 'Em by relying on my time at deep position to take my shot, IF I have the hands. If I have aces or kings wired on my first two cards, I call regardless of where I'm sitting. But if the flop kicks over that third ace or king, you can be sure I'm banging out a raise. I play very strong when I have high trips or a flush right after the flop.

My theory is to make the table pay when I am loaded and run when I have a good or decent hand and there are multiple raises. You can't win the Kentucky Derby with a plow horse and you can't win Hold 'Em hands with weak cards.

Again, I play against players who bet cautiously and raise when I see them bobbing and weaving, counting their chips constantly, or showing a penchant to fold with any type raise against them. You ain't gonna chase me when I have a good hand but I do respect a strong player who shows a pattern of raising when he is powerful. Then I'll fold.

You can't have an ego in this game. If you're not sure about your low trips or possible flush and are facing heavy raises from late position players, you gotta toss in the hand.

But, and I told you this earlier in the book, stay focused on that raiser to pick up his pattern of play and whether he was on the come or definitely loaded early. Poker players run their own patterns of play and you gotta pick them up. Develop your own theory of play and vary it only to avoid being stereotyped. In my opinion, you should:

Get aggressive when in deep position.
Don't chase.
Read other players and pick out constant raisers and make them pay when you are loaded.
Play cautiously when in poor early betting positions.
Read possible combinations from the flop and turn card and match with your hand.
Don't get in a bidding war when you're not loaded.
Don't chase pots when value is low and you are called on to match a couple of raises with only a decent hand.
Bet aggressive early if you are loaded. Don't keep players around to build the pot.
Don't be afraid to fold when combinations against you are many, you're faced with multiple raises and you have only a good hand.
NEVER show your hand or give away your theories.

You will develop your own pattern of play which you vary only 10 percent of the time to throw off opponents. Or have I said that before?

70

Raising Intelligently

This is my advice on when to raise:

> Never after first two cards, even as DD with pair of aces
> After the flop when you have trips, straight, flush, boat, or two single pairs in late betting position
> After the turn card when you have straight, flush, boat, and there is no pair on board, with trips, sitting medium deep, to deep position
> In early positions with power hand after the flop or turn card if I have high flush or better will reraise with boat, even in early position
> Cautiously when loaded if you have full house but board shows pair higher than your set of trips

Someone will say: "I raise every time I'm loaded." Now you've got it! I wanna get out all hangers-on when I'm strong and will reraise if I have boat and there's no pair on board higher than my trips.

I do not raise on the come when there are six or more players left in the game and my hand could only be labeled good—low straight, 10-high flush or lower, two pairs, etc. This game eventually turns into a raising war so you'll get used to seeing higher flushes, full boats, and four of a kind beating your strong hands.

Don't make raising be the most important part of your arsenal. Use it as a tool to: get hangers-on out when you're strong, build up the pot when you're powerful, or send a message when you're deep in a position seat, have a good hand, and there are no pairs on board.

Again, once you get the feel of this game, you'll develop your own patterns. But realize what you're up against before it starts to shock you when you see a succession of power hands turn up after you've been raising heavily since the flop. Pick your spots to raise and do it for the reasons listed.

71

The River

Before I go back over some theories as to what to look for in this game, let's finish with the river card, the last card turned over.

Now comes the betting and raising by all those who believe they have a high hidden hand, and of course, by those sitting in the deep positions. That's why it is so vastly important to read the possible hands against you after the flop. If you don't learn to properly gauge the competition and read the possibilities, along with evaluating your cards, you're gonna get whacked. By checking out all possibile combinations that could beat you, plus watching the betting patterns of the other players, you'll have an idea how you stand as the game progresses to the late stages.

I remind you of the power of position play in this game and all good players learn how to take advantage of it. Your job is to look for and evaluate these moves. The river card ignites raising in this game, so don't reach this point with a water pistol. Very seldom will you be able to pull a bluff with even a fairly weak set of five cards on board. Usually somebody has something.

A good player sitting under the gun is gonna play tight because of his lousy position. Let's say that after the flop, which is KS, 10S, 8H, he calls the initial bet, then the last player raises and the early round player comes back with his own raise. A good player in an early position ain't gonna raise unless he has a strong hand. I would immediately read him for two kings in the hole, or at worst, two spades, one of them high.

If I'm sitting with a pair of jacks, queens, or lower, I'm gone.

No good player raises this early from the weak positions, so you gotta read him as loaded, especially since he is not worried about a reraise from the deep player. If he is banging a raise this early, right after the flop, he's got something strong. If he doesn't, at least he got his message out that he's alive in this game and even the deep players will hesitate taking him on with a reraise.

At seventh street, the raise will come only from the players who either caught their strong hand or who had it after the turn card and now want maximum value. Good players rarely bluff on seventh street. It is too late to be of any value because if a player is strong, he's gonna call that raise, so the bluff is wasted money. You'll see good players raising on seventh street when they are loaded, have pretty close to a lock hand, and have four to six players still involved. They're looking for value. A player sitting with trips on seventh street surely ain't raising with only one other player involved and positively not if the board shows a pair higher than the amount of his trips. There ain't no value in that raise.

For some strange reason, poor or mediocre players think that just because they reached the river card and have a good hand, it is mandatory to raise just to pick up a few extra chips.

It all goes back to reading the players, their bets, their patterns, your hand, the five cards on board, the pattern of betting for that hand, and the value of the pot weighed against your raise which may invite a reraise from a hand stronger than yours.

At seventh street you get the chance to evaluate all these things because you're staring at five of the seven cards your opponent has.

72

Power of Observation

I've been playing poker since Adam and Eve were childless and Texas Hold 'Em since it was the new kid in town. My theory is the same as in seven-card stud because Texas Hold 'Em also is played by poker players and most of these have flaws.

Obviously, you can't see their two first cards but you can pick up on tells which give you an idea of what they MAY have.

This is done by observing their betting actions after the flop, hesitations in making a move and all the little things we went over in the seven-card stud section.

In Hold 'Em, you have good players aware of the power of deep positions, raising at the right times, and checking or calling in the early seats. If you have, for example, a pair of queens, a raise invites a comeback from a deep position player and you don't know if he is loaded or just using that advantage seat to see if you respond. We know all these things, but the late position player still makes this tiny mistake.

A player who is sitting under the gun with a pair of jacks when the flop turns over AD, KC, QS, will check and the next four players will do likewise. The player in the sixth seat bets the minimum and the DD (last player) calls. He is broadcasting to the world he has nothing. He is leaving four to six players in for another card with a tiny bet. If he had something, he would raise, at least to get out a couple of players but more to give the impression he had something. If that were me, I'd fold if I had nothing because the raise could stir a reraise from the early players who had to check and there I'd be, sitting with garbage, a stupid raise, and the need to call a raise just to stick around.

Right away you pick up the dumb move by the player in the sixth seat who should have bet the maximum. Both late players made mistakes. One stayed in with nothing, making a small bet and allowing early players to bang back. The other called a small bet when the move screamed for a raise or fold. The right move would have been for both these late players to check and at least get a free card. They surely blurted out to the competition that they were weak and probably didn't even have at least a high pair.

It is absolutely mandatory that you observe every tiny factor you can in these games. The way a player bets after the flop doesn't necessarily give you an edge on what his first two cards are, but the turn card should shed some light. With the turn card you'll know if a straight or flush is possible and if a pair is on board, signaling that a full house could be made.

Players in the early seats now betting big is an indication they have a strong hand. If you are equally strong, bang right back. If you are weak, respect the possibilities and fold. If you have a good hand in deep position but fear too many possibilities of better hands, call but DO NOT go to the river on the come, especially with a pair on board and one or two raises already banged out.

Hold 'Em is playing your hand but also trying to find flaws in your adversaries. They're there, but you gotta pick them up.

73

Reality

I've played Hold 'Em with great players, good players, bad players, and lousy players. I've been beaten by good players but also by poor players when I had the cards but ended up second best. In the early days of my poker playing I always thought I could win every hand. That's wrong and that is why bad poker players lose so much... they stay too long.

It takes me no more than seven or eight hands to find out where my competition for that session is gonna come from. I try to find weaknesses in the play of these good opponents because they are capable of beating me. The lousy, bad, and poor players are easy. In the long run, their mistakes become costly as all the strong players pick up on these weaknesses and use them against the patsy.

You ain't gonna become a great player overnight. It's gonna take many sessions, and yes, losses to get a feel for this game. I can make you aware of what to look for but it's up to you to be able to do it. You ain't gonna win every hand, so get that into your noggin right now. The idea is to get out of hands when it is apparent you are beat and make the most of hands when you're loaded. Try starting off in lower-stakes games to try to acquire the feel for the game. It's there, but you gotta cultivate it.

The reality of it all is that no matter how good you are, there is someone better or at least as good in the same game and he wants your money. Some advice:

Don't play tight.

Don't play loose.
Don't talk.
Don't have tells.
Don't gloat.
Don't show your hands.
Don't think bluffing is a way of life in poker.
Don't show emotion whether you win or lose.
Don't expect to win every hand.
Don't stay in when you're obviously weak.
Don't raise all the time, regardless of seat position.
Don't be afraid to drop.
Don't be afraid to check.
Don't think you're the best player in the world, even though you may become it.
Don't think that if you do become the best player you should win every hand. You can't and you won't!

I think you have an idea of the strategy of Hold 'Em. The next section goes over some money management moves.

Money Management

74

Hold 'Em: Money Management

We now slide into the section that is more important than any knowledge you may gain about Hold 'Em, or for that matter, any form of gambling. A lot of you are nodding and acting like you agree with that sentence. Well then, why don't you do something about it?

You all admit that you know about money management and want money management and will try to manage your money at the tables. But as soon as you park your carcass on one of those casino stools, it's as if you're sitting on your brains.

I could give you 7,643 different examples of different hands that will occur during a poker session but there would still would be 7,644 I left out. After a while you'd just be trying to digest all the examples and would start skipping over the analysis, so I won't bore you with all that gibberish. I've read books by sharp, excellent Hold 'Em players and they give out all types of percentages and odds and examples, and it all seems and sounds so logical.

But I disagree with a lot of that stuff on odds. If I'm sitting with KH, QH, and the flop shows JH, 5H, 5C, I now have four hearts to a flush. The geniuses of the world spit out a percentage or odds against your catching that flush. If there are eight other players in the game and three cards have already been buried, how the heck do I know how many hearts are already used up in their hands. Plus there's more than a deck left undealt that may or may not have a lot of hearts left in it. How can you calculate your chances without knowing how many other players are sitting with two hearts and also have four of those love cards?

Suppose you're early in a position seat and you check. In back of you come three successive raises and in a $5–$10 game, it is now gonna cost you $30 to look at the turn card and surely another set of raises. Are you gonna call? No way. Regardless of what the odds say, I'm gone. Those two fives scare me, as does the fact that the ace of hearts is unaccounted for. It's conservative and it's money management.

Odds and percentages, in my opinion, rate far down the road in comparison to protecting your money. You don't read a book on how to ride a bicycle and then enter a cross-country jaunt. You don't read a book on computers, then sit down and build a competitor to the space system. You don't read a book on sex, then dial Pamela Sue Anderson for a date." And you don't read a book on Hold 'Em and enter the World Championship in Las Vegas.

You learn the game, the basics, the theory, and you learn to read players. You practice reading three-card flops then you play a casino game of $1–$3 or $3–$6 Hold 'Em. You learn the logical moves by being subjected to them and you learn how to manage your money!

The last part of that sentence says it all.... WERE YOU LISTENING?

75

Hold 'Em: Need

I'm gonna list some of the reasons people gamble. See if you can find yourself. People gamble:

for money
for excitement
for an outlet
for the chase
to be part of the ambiance of casino life
to be around people
to win money to change their lives
to pay bills
to send kids to college
to give their families things that don't come through normal financial earnings

Most of these center around money and all of them zero in on the four-letter title of this chapter: NEED.

If you see yourself in any of those examples, you could probably preface the words with "I need." Nothing wrong with that, but the manner in which we seek to get that financial payoff usually dims our senses and kicks off aggressive moves that we would not normally use in our everyday life.

Susie Q loves poker and goes to the casino a couple of times a week to play Hold 'Em. First, she does her shopping, bringing along a handful of coupons she clipped out of the paper and a hand-held computer to make sure she doesn't exceed the $84 she is setting aside for groceries. Then she heads for the tables and eventually gets involved in a $5–$10 Hold 'Em game. She is dealt JD, QD, and then the flop shows 10D, 10S, 9S, and two raises to Susie Q.

She calls and the turn card is an 8S, giving her a straight but leaving a ton of options on board for seven players still in the game. Betting has been heavy and with the river card to go, the biggest pot of the night is waiting to be plucked. The last card is KS, and Susie Q is still around with her straight. Susie Q, who patted herself on the back for saving $1.32 at the supermarket by buying off-brands peas, is now calling every bet and raise in sight.

A half-baked newcomer to Hold 'Em can see that the straight and other possibilities for Susie Q, are tremendously out-weighed by the possible power hands of the other contestants. But Susie Q only sees that ever growing pot and envisions that bonanza coming her way. Money management, not to mention logic, brains, and skill go out the window. Of course, she eventually loses the pot. She had a straight but didn't read the obvious flush on board.

We all go through these periods at the table where "ah, just let me take this shot!" goes through our minds and we forsake all control and go for the kill. It's happened to me, to every person I know, and it'll happen to you. Sure, I cringe when it's time to surrender a real good hand when a big pot is sitting a foot away. But if I read I'm beat, it's more sensible to save my money for the time when I'm in the driver's seat.

It's called money management and it relates to the title of this chapter: You NEED it!

76

Hold 'Em: Playing Tight

We've already covered the rocks or tight players at a poker table and a lot of times these are pros who bet only when they got the goods. You can't blame them because their whole income depends on the money they win. I am a super conservative player but vary my betting to thwart the chances of someone zeroing in on my play. There is a difference between betting tight and betting smart. The reason you're reading this book is to get even a tiny edge in winning money at poker.

I told you that reading player patterns is one of the biggest attributes of successful poker players. I ain't gonna change that. The purpose of this chapter is to reemphasize betting smart. Sure I repeat these messages, but if I believed you grasped them the first time around, I wouldn't have to. I know you weren't listening then and it's only 20-80 you are now.

You're dealt 10D, JD and call from a deep position. The flop shows 9C, 9S, 7D, and two raises are in front of you. Let's say you know that one of those raises was a good player. Why is he becoming so aggressive so early in a lousy position?

Think, now, think! The answer is right on the table in the flop. You've got to read him for the third 9. A good player, when he has the goods early, will send out a message, even from the poor seats. He has his trips or else he just calls. No good player blows money on the come this early with a medium pair. You know he hasn't got his straight or flush and he isn't raising to kick out players who checked in front of him.

You have three diamonds and an open gut straight. Based on

those raises, you're in trouble. Even just calling and cutting off future raises for this round ain't worth the price just to see the turn card. Money management is the prime reason to drop, backed by the fact you see yourself as being beat this early. You are surely on the come, so at this point there is little value in staying around. This does not qualify you as a rock because you are getting out early even though you are in a good position seat.

Bad poker players risk their money at this point. Good poker players know how to preserve that bankroll for the times they have the tools. You ain't gonna win every hand and in this particular case, cutting losses is more important.

77

Do You Want Money Management?

I've read a lot of books, watched videos, studied theorics, and attended lectures by poker experts, of whom you have undoubtedly heard. I won't mention their names for fear of inadvertently leaving someone out. These people are all sharp poker players, either in stud or Hold 'Em. They are successful because they adopted a method of play that is comfortable because it works for them.

Your job is to pick the type of poker you wish to concentrate on, master it, add your own theories, and keep adjusting until you zero in on the type of play that works for you. It is my humble opinion that my style is great, but it may be too conservative for many of you. Add your own ideas.

Remember that statement I mentioned earlier in the book that I believe is mandatory adoption for every gambler. Here it is again: "It's not how much you win that's important...it's how little you lose that counts!"

Man, I hope you catch the drift of that little sentence. It has helped me tremendously. I ain't gonna go banging in raises with my full boat of threes and sixes if I see a pair of jacks on the board and two or three jackals in the bushes, meeting all my bets. Sure I'd like to make that boat count and run up the pot. But if someone else has jacks or better over a pair in a higher hand, it's gonna cost me some green. So I pull in my aggressive tendencies and concentrate on cutting potential losses. If a pair of jacks is on board, someone could have another jack and my boat is dropping in value.

Some of these other teachers of poker consider knowledge of the game more important and certain moves more effective than reducing losses. I vehemently disagree. They ain't wrong. It's just that our styles differ. My emphasis on gambling is geared more to reducing losses, accepting small wins, and using impeccable discipline.

Naturally, people reading, adjusting my play to offset their zeroing in on my pattern, and reverse bluffing is part of my arsenal. But someday you'll see that money management is more important than strategy.

78

Poker: Betting Moves

I used a term called "reverse bluffing" in the previous chapter and many of you picked up on what it is. For those who didn't, it has to do with changing your betting style to avoid being typecast.

All night long, in this particular session of seven-card stud, you've been checking or calling on fourth street, even with a pair on board. The other players read you as being not too strong and watch for the end of each game to get a read on whether you had trips or at least a couple of pairs. You "accidentally" allow them to see your cards, but only occasionally, to set up their opinions for later. On this night, you haven't had that set of trips or any strong hand. The other sharp players make a mental note of that.

Later you have a pair of fours and this time you raise and reraise. Since you have previously let them see your cards, the sharpies figure you are bluffing to get them to make their moves. The readers stay in and don't fall for your bluff. At the end of the hand you turn over four fours or a full house that you had early and disrupt their erroneous read on your previous play.

Reverse bluffing is merely reversing your pattern of play to further attempt to discourage being read by sharp players who must find a flaw in the armor of as many players as they can. Get these strong players to THINK you're doing something, while all the while you're THINKING of things to change the way they THINK you're THINKING. I THINK you THINK I don't know what I'm THINKING about. But if you THINK I'm gonna sit down and get into your THINK tank, you've got another THINK coming.

And I THINK you get the message. But I also get that sinking feeling in my gut that you THINK I've sunk to lower levels to get you to THINK more than you THINK you should.

Maybe I have... but see how hard it is to read my purpose?

79

Poker: Odds

You ain't gonna get me to offer a chapter on the odds to catch such and such a card or the odds of winning a pot based on a mathematical law of probability that only a handful of geniuses can work out anyway. I deal with logic in poker and odds be hanged because I don't understand them and most of you reading this book ain't gonna grasp it anyhow.

I give seminars all over the country, appear on radio talk shows approximately ten to twelve times a week, and participate in pay-per-view TV programs on all types of gambling. Sports betting is by far my favorite, poker next, then casino games, and I am quite proficient in all. What does being so smart at all these games do for me? It cuts my losses, makes me aware of streaks, and allows me to grind out a profit 60 percent to 65 percent of the time. I haven't a clue what my odds are of winning from a standpoint of measuring my hand against my opponent's.

You'll hear many theories. One would be if you have a fair hand in Hold 'Em such as a KH, QD, and the flop shows 10C, 6D, 6S when you're the DD, deep in a strong position with all calls in front of you, a smart move is to raise. NO WAY! In this case, the lousy flop didn't help you and a strong position doesn't make up for poor cards. The move is to just drop. It's poor money management to use your position to make a dumb raise or call, especially when there are five to seven players in front of you.

You'll also hear some mathematical wizard say he'll call a bet on fifth street when the pot is heavy with prior raises and his odds of winning have increased because there are no fours showing and his pair of fours has now shifted the odds in his favor. Again I disagree. The size of the pot may be tempting but I ain't pouring good money after that dream regardless of an illogical thought that my odds of catching trips have increased.

You can't win every hand of poker and you can't stay in every hand if you intend to be successful at poker.

How I hate that word *odds!*

80

Hold 'Em: Playing Loose or Tight?

Here's a question I get asked constantly and yet it's not a bad one: "Do all good players, like the real pros, constantly raise the other players or are they tight players who make rocks seem like putty?" Two good points.

First, no good player and certainly no pro plays the same way all the time. Sure you should raise when you've got the goods and make the other players pay for your good fortune. You should also raise to put notions in the heads of good players who are trying to read your moves. No, pros do not try to steal pots by raising all the time.

Remember this statement: Flat betting stinks and will NEVER be profitable!

This is especially true in even chance casino games such as blackjack and baccarat, with outside bets in roulette, place betting the 6 and 8 in craps, and in all types of sports betting. Betting $5 or $10 or $50 or $100 hand after hand is flat betting and you gotta lose eventually. You gotta go up when you're in a streak, yet thousands of players refuse to move off that original bet and sooner or later will get beat.

Flat betting in poker has this drawback: If you constantly call, you'll never win enough with your good hands to make up for those you'll lose when you're second or third best.

Of course, you should raise to take advantage of your good

hands and build the pot, to send a message, and to slow down a constant raiser. You must learn when to raise because it's always done for a purpose. DON'T flat bet.

The second part of that original question is a definite NO. All pros do not play tight. They surely don't play crazy because it ain't as if they won't be in another game for three or four more months. They'll be back in action several hours later and probably the next day. Even a perfect player can only logically expect to win 65 percent to 70 percent of the time. So if he doesn't have the cards, he realizes it may be a bad run and he'll pull back until the bad streak is over. But the pros absolutely do not acquire a pattern of constant tight play.

You vary your bets, adjust your style, don't go for gigantic paydays, and accept small wins. That is what all sharp pros have in common.

81

Hold 'Em: Betting Patterns

Swinging back to Hold 'Em, the same theory of betting crazy versus to betting smart should be weighed. Good players in Hold 'Em soon zero in on other good players and try like mad to read their moves.

Suppose you're dealt a jack and queen of hearts and you're sitting in deep position. The flop shows 7C, 7S, 9D, none of which helps you directly. There is a minimum bet and five calls come to you with no one to your left. If you call, you've sent a message to the world that you ain't got a 7 because with deep position and fifth street, you're surely gonna get rid of some players with a raise. With a call you send out a signal as to how weak you are.

So proper money management is a quick raise. It's doubtful you'll get a reraise with that garbage and if you don't get raised by someone sitting with aces or kings, you're sitting in a good position. This is one of the few times I'll raise with a poor hand. But a message has been sent and curtails any reraises from others also on the fence.

Let's get to you being one of the blinds, with a medium pair of tens (10C, 10H) dealt. The flop shows 8C, 7D, 2S, and only a raise from the DD breaks up six calls and two drops. I'll reraise from my weak position and surely will chase some hanger-on. If the raiser comes back, I simply call. If he doesn't reraise, I may be sitting high. It also gets him thinking. It's a form of money management because if the DD doesn't get raised, he's sure to start banging the pot after the turn card.

Sometimes a money management move doesn't necessarily mean keeping your chips in front of you. It could be a raise. I've already told you that in regular seven-card stud I want my hand by fifth street or I'm looking for the exit door. These are my basic rules:

Call on third street 95 percent of the time; rarely raise.
Use fourth street as raising street if have two pairs, trips, or four cards to a flush.
Call with a decent hand on fifth street or run.

I follow these patterns about 80 percent of the time, unless I send out a message raise or check and raise to open some brain waves in the good players, to get them thinking.

Finally, here's another statement that will bring angry disagreement from other pros: I do not stay in a pot with a poor hand or even a half-decent hand when the pile of chips in the center of the table would pay off the budget deficit of New York City. I don't stay in because of an oversized pot when I am weak. The size of the pot does not dictate my play. Very rarely will you win a pot with a subpar hand. So why toss your money away simply because those chips look so tempting?

82

Drawing to Dead Hands

Suppose in Hold 'Em you're dealt QC and JH, middle position, and the flop shows KD, 8D, 3D. You need two diamonds on board to catch a flush and that's only a tie with everyone else, not counting someone already sitting with a higher diamond. Even if a queen or jack of diamonds shows, you're paired but in a lot of trouble.

There is absolutely no reason to stay in. You're drawing to a dead hand where only a super turn and river card can give you a shot. Get out.

There is a rule of thumb that you should play as often as you can when in deep positions, but there have to be exceptions. I won't draw to dead hands or even call raises with weak or semiweak hands, regardless of my position. Some excellent Hold 'Em players let it all hang out when they have strong positions and weak hands. I disagree. You gotta make that decision on your own, but I just don't believe in chasing with garbage.

Now, let's get to the theory of playing a hand, depending on the number of players left after the flop.

If I have the cards and there are nine players left and multiple raises, I'm playing my hand as to its value based on where I perceive myself to be in relation to the opposition. I also do not stay with weak or only semidecent hands because there's only one or two other players left and both of them seem weak. I can't cut a tree with a wet noodle and I'll rarely steal a pot with a weak hand.

The number of players remaining in the game is not a factor. My hand is the key, as linked with the flop. Now that's a logical statement and as you get deeper into poker, you'll see that many answers to your questions require only a logical evaluation.

83

Money Management:
Is It Important?

A part of money management has to do with the way you play, so knowledge of the game and money management actually go hand-in-hand in all aspects of poker.

I've talked about the necessity of controlling your bankroll by realizing you absolutely cannot win every hand, so you gotta have the brains and guts to fold even in those hands where you are strong, but it is obvious the other guy is stronger.

So cut your losses by getting out of hands in which you feel you're beat and show absolutely no emotion whatsoever. If you lose, show a blank stare. And if you win, don't go giving high fives like those jerks in the NBA who give a high five to a teammate who MISSES a foul shot. Or how about in the NFL when on the first play of the game a running back slips in the backfield and some 330-pound tackle falls on top of him. Then the rest of the team goes nuts patting this guy on the back. Real jerks who act like jerks. Don't do this in poker. Show nothing that might indicate you are susceptible to any type of emotion.

Knowing how to read players, when to drop, when to raise, how to avoid tells, and being sure you have something on fifth street before going further in the hand are all part of money management. Way back in the seven-card stud section, I went deep into the idea of leaving on fifth street when you ain't strong. Same is true in Hold 'Em, where I use the flop to determine if I'm strong enough to go on.

Here are some hints to use playing Texas Hold 'Em:

Call on first two cards if you're good (see chapter sixty-one on suggested rating of hands).
Become aggressive when in deep position.
Raise in deep position after the flop, if good or decent.
Don't chase after the flop.

And here are some tips for poker:

Call rather than raise on first three cards.
Use raises at fourth street.
Decide to fold at fifth street if not strong.
Use raises again at sixth street.
Using raises at seventh street is not mandatory because you ain't gonna get out anybody who has a good hand.

The suggestions on poker pertain to seven-card stud and hi/lo.

It may sound like these are knowledge moves but they ain't. They are money management moves! Are they important? More than you realize right now.

84

Winding Down Money Management

Let's say you're in a Hold 'Em game of $10–$20, sitting with a pair of jacks wired. Pretty good hand. The flop shows AC, QC, 6C. Nothing helped you and now three clubs and two higher cards are staring you in the face. Regardless of position, it is a money management move to fold. There is no question you're in deep trouble and this move is obvious even if you're a novice. The reason you drop is to save money because it's definitely gonna get more expensive to stay. You'll hear many pros state that money management is not as important in poker as it is in other games. Are they nuts?

You've gotta read the difference between knowledge and money management. Talking at the table is a prelude to tells. Eventually a sharp player will pick up your stupid chatter and read something out of it that'll hurt you. That's knowledge.

Don't talk about what you need or don't need or anything else pertaining to whether you have a lock or need a card or other gibberish. That's knowledge.

Play poker and shut your mouth. That's knowledge and has nothing to do with money management.

I've already gone over bluffing, which is a small part of poker and not the big part many people think. If you can pull off one bluff a game, you're a genius and ought to run for president. But we've already got a bluffer in that position who is an expert, so

179

you'll have to put that talent in another direction. Same with raises. You don't raise every time you get a good hand. You raise to find out what the opposition will do and to send a message. These are tools that you can use to improve your game, cut losses, and improve your chances of winning.

It doesn't take a genius to realize when you're getting beat at a poker table. If you bought in for $100 and in an hour you're down to $30 and getting absolutely rotten starting hands, what are you doing at that table? The stupid statement "the cards will change" should be coming out of the mouth of a two-year-old. Sure they'll change, maybe they'll get worse. Or maybe they won't change for another hour. Are you gonna sit there and get whacked and blow your whole stake? Managing your money also has to do with protecting it when things are going bad.

Will you listen to these tiny hints? I wonder... it ain't gonna be easy.

85

Wrapping Up Money Management

Guess you got an idea what money management is and how it applies to all forms of gambling and to poker in this instance. When I hear a so-called poker expert say money management in poker is overrated, it's obvious that this guy is full of bull-oney!

My theory is to cut losses and get out of hands when I read that I'm beat. I won't risk more money when I'm not sitting with a strong hand and the opposition appears strong. Money management is carried into the game itself and has to do with your becoming proficient in reading the cards on the table and how they relate to your chances of winning or losing.

Poker is a great game because you can keep moving from table to table until you settle in on a session where you are superior to the other players. You don't have to and shouldn't play with players who are superior to you. These sharks will have you for dinner.

You can play in lower-stake games until you are proficient and then start to move up the ladder.

Q: When will you know you're ready for the bigger games?
A: When you are winning consistently at lower-stake games and have become perfect in analyzing all types of situations.

Stop thinking of poker as the "big kill" game. You're gonna

run into plenty of people who have the same goal in mind that you do—WIN MONEY!

Don't PRACTICE the theories I teach you about money management... DO them. Have the guts to make yourself a strong player.

It starts and ends with money management!

Discipline

86

Discipline

I've told you before about the ten books I've written and my twenty-three videotapes that cover every facet of gambling. In those books and tapes I teach the game itself but then gear every single bit of energy into trying to get you to learn discipline. That's what's gonna decide whether you win or lose.

Sure skills are important, but a donkey could sit at a table, win the first eight hands, get ahead $1,280 and not know enough to quit. That's because he's a jackass. A human being could sit at a table, get ahead $1,280 and KNOW it's time to quit. Of course, he doesn't quit and that's why he's also a jackass.

When do you know that it's time to quit? That's a good question, glad you asked.

In poker, unlike casino games, the amount of the pot is always higher than the amount you invest per hand, so the rules deviate from blackjack, for instance, when you receive back an amount equal to your bet. The method you will use is called "guarantee and excess." It is not necessarily the same percentage for every player but the theory of quitting a winner is still mandatory.

If you double your starting stake, you're in fabulous shape, so I'm gonna back down to a 70 percent win goal, which is repeated in the next chapter. Just think of the number 70 and fix it in your mind. If you start with $100 at a session and get ahead $70, you have reached your goal.

Now the tough part!

87

Win Goal

OK, we've settled on a win goal of 70 percent. The next chapter tells you what to do with your profit, so right now we'll touch on the reason you set a goal in the first place.

How the deuce can you determine when it's time to leave a table if you don't preset an amount of money you should get ahead based on your session money?

It all goes back to the reason you're gambling in the first place—money.

My friend E. Z. Lyer is an out-and-out liar. He tells his wife he's gonna play until he has enough to take her to a nice restaurant for dinner. E. Z. Lyer gets ahead $600 with a $100 buy-in and starts chasing every pot as if he is destined to go undefeated for the afternoon. His win goal is reached, passed, and ignored as this goof thinks he's the first person to hit a scorching hot streak. He originally wanted to get ahead $60 but now he's closing in on $600. He'll see $60 profit again, but on his way back to zero as he runs into a string of bad cards.

Does he stop at the $60 profit the second time around? No way, now he wants to get back to $600. This guy hasn't got a goal in his head, he has a hole in his head. E. Z. Lyer lies when he says he'll quit when he gets ahead $60. He doesn't have the guts to quit.

Do you see yourself somewhere in that story?

The next chapter tells you what he SHOULD have done!

88

Guarantee and Excess

That dope E. Z. Lyer should have set his win goal and when he reached it, jumped into the discipline move of guarantee and excess.

Let's say he agrees with my thinking and sets 70 percent as his goal. I ain't telling him to leave the game, that would be stupid.

Look at how easy it is:

1. Rat-hole your starting session money, in this case $100.
2. Put aside 50 percent of the profit of $70 ($35), called your guarantee.
3. Continue to play with the other ($35) called the Excess.

What's so hard about that move? You've made sure your starting bankroll of $100 is intact, plus you've guaranteed that even if you lose the excess, you've got $35 to bring home.

Notice I did not take you out of the game. That is the misconception people have about discipline. Setting win goals is merely putting up a point at which you set aside the guarantee that surely goes home with you because it absolutely cannot be touched again.

Once you decide on your win goal you can't deviate. The amount you set is up to you. Maybe 70 percent is too high or too low, that's your decision. But what a great feeling to know your starting session money is intact along with a guaranteed profit.

Go back and dwell on the best sentence in this book and how

it applies to all gamblers. Do you remember it? Of course you don't! "Seventy Percent of all the people who enter a casino get ahead, yet 90 percent of that 70 percent give the profit back."

Memorize it. You may be one of the people starring in that percentage.

89

Handling the Excess

Once you hit your win goal and put the guarantee away, I didn't tell you to leave the table. Never leave a winning session! Stay in action with the other half of that win goal, called the excess. This money stays on the table as your session amount and since the casinos usually offer table stakes, you cannot dip into that guarantee to put additional money at risk.

If you reach a pot where your excess is down to zippo, you merely play all in. If you lose, that session is over. You should quit for the day with that guarantee or at least move to another table. The one you're at is drying up as far as you are concerned, so it's time to leave.

However, let's say you are playing with your excess and win a $36 pot. When you pull that profit to you, divide it in half. Put 50 percent ($18) with your guarantee and keep 50 percent with the excess. Every subsequent winning pot is divided in half. This way you are increasing your guarantee while at the same time increasing your excess. You stay at the table until the excess is gone.

Since you cannot remove a chip or add money or chips to your session amount during a hand, you must rat-hole 50 percent of that winning pot to the guarantee in between deals. Definitely get that money off the table or else it will have to be used during a subsequent hand and I DO NOT want you touching your guarantee again at that session.

Handling the excess is merely the act or art, if you will, of increasing the amount of money you'll leave that session with. Will you do this?

Show me!

90

Can You Do It?

The answer to that question is gonna result in a lot of affirmative nodding from people reading this page. But the actual truth of the matter is that you won't or can't do it because it's too hard, too restrictive, too conservative.

How hard is it to get in the habit of setting aside profits which will eventually be yours?

I ain't asking you to restrict anything. You're still playing while at the same time building up your guaranteed profits. People put savings away in real life all the time. Finally, why do you consider it conservative? Nothing has changed in your overall playing strategy. Conservative is not an issue with this move.

Just go back over the process and catch what I'm trying to do. It has the moves of the Little Three: theory, logic and trends. My theory is that if you get ahead at a table, don't give it back. Ain't it logical to guarantee yourself a profit after you prove you can get ahead in a game? And by playing with the excess, you're staying at a table where you've been in a hot trend.

I don't know if you can handle this act of discipline. The pros do it, and while they don't win all the time, you can be sure they win 65 percent to 75 percent of their sessions.

91

Loss Limits Again

Yeah, yeah, I know I already wrote a chapter on loss limits and kept repeating the message over and over that it ain't important how much you win, it's important how little you lose.

Well we're down to the final pages of this book and I wonder if this message has settled into a prominent place in your brain, or has it already entered one ear and shot through that empty cavern and right out the other?

Loss limits are important to the pros because if they don't put a ceiling on how much they lose in a certain month, week, day, or session, they'd better start scanning the want ads for the start of another stake. That thought is repulsive to me, so I set strong, disciplined, intelligent loss limits.

The bad part of this chapter is that some of you will look at it as being just another repeat of the same old tired garbage. The good part of this chapter is that maybe two or three additional converts will have the light go on and finally see what I'm saying. Or is it hear what I'm saying? I'm not too good in grammar. My strong points in school were jim, hisstorie, and speleng.

92

Accepting Small Returns

Every time I do a TV or radio guest appearance or conduct a lecture on gambling, the host will close with the obligatory question: "Do you have a specific message you would like to leave with our listeners?"

Every time I say the same thing. When it comes to gambling, the two most important parts of your play are to set and follow intelligent loss limits and accept small returns.

We've already beaten the loss limit situation to death so let's spend a little time on accepting small returns.

For some reason most people think a gambling session is a failure unless you walk away with a four-figure return. They gotta be nuts. It is my humble opinion that a successful gambling session is walking away with more money than I started with. I don't care how much I win. I care how little I lose. Or have I said that before?

Today is a hot Friday morning in June and I am jotting down a few chapters before taking that two-and-a-half-hour drive to Atlantic City, where I will attempt to win a day's pay. I drive to my mother's house, pick her up, and make the trip. I play Pai Gow poker for four hours, win $106 and start the jaunt back. Counting gas, tolls, and a stop for ice cream (I'm a big spender), my net return is $78.

My bankroll was $3,000 and my profit $78, which comes to a winning percentage of 0.26 percent for the casino end of my day. I won another $104 in baseball sports betting when a Round Robin covered the loss of a blown parlay and a shot at the

NBA finals. (I had Seattle getting the points, which of course lost.) Altogether my day, which covered noon to 12:30 A.M., kicked off a $182 profit and .05 percent return on the money I started with, even though a loss limit was involved.

With that colossal return of $182 I slept like a baby, content in the fact that the day was a success, not a failure.

Even had I broken even in the baseball game, the $78 net return in Pai Gow poker would have resulted in the same relaxed feeling because I didn't lose!

During that casino trip, I was down almost $300 a couple of times and contemplating packing it in. A strong finish gave me a profit and I was ecstatic. The key was accepting small returns!

Will you do it? Can you do it? I doubt it!

Should you do it? Do you really need me to give you that answer?

You'd BETTER do it!

93

Reality

My whole theory of gambling is wrapped up in that last chapter. It is everything you need to know about discipline. Some of you will scoff and say I made that story up just to prove a point. No, I didn't. I don't gotta make up stories to try and get across my messages. Most of you are walking examples of how stupid people play.

How many of you have gotten ahead 30 percent, 40 percent, 50 percent of your starting bankroll and given the money back... plus the money you started with? I'd be the first with my hands in the air, admitting to be one of those dorks. It took me years to grasp the reality of gambling—that if you are perfect you have a 50-50 chance of winning.

Did you grasp that word *perfect*? That means you know everything about the game you're playing. And still your chances never exceed 50 percent.

I'm a perfect poker player. I know all the right moves to make (based on my conservative theory), have the bankroll, have excellent money management and discipline techniques, and still I strive to merely make a day's pay. I've played with other poker pros who are perfect players. Why can't we win all the time if we're so good? Because the game offers only a 50-50 chance... if you're perfect and have all facets of the Big Four and Little Three.

That's the reality of gambling!

Are you a perfect player? Do you have the Big four and Little three and all the other necessities mentioned in this book that make you a perfect player? Well if you don't, you'd better get them if you intend to be consistently successful at poker. That's the out-and-out reality of it.

94

The Professional
Poker Player

A few chapters back I told you to check out the theories of other pro poker players who have written books on this subject, not because I think they know more than me but because their theories differ from mine and you may like some of their ideas. I told you this book was aimed at the intermediate player, not the beginner or pro. There are books available that go deeper into the games we covered and you might like to read the thoughts of these other pros. When the time is right, I'll write a book on advanced poker. Omaha hi/lo, Pineapple, and all the other Hold 'Em games that are popping up.

If you've ever been to Las Vegas, you've probably seen the jam-packed poker rooms going all day long. There are professional poker players at these tables, usually at the mid- or high-level games. No, I don't want you to take them on. Wait until you have mastered the art of beating the player at the low stakes tables.

Many years ago, I entered every tournament in Las Vegas, trying to win the biggie. I never won a major tournament because in those days I was just starting out and was not in the league of those pros who took me to task. I did win many smaller tournaments and daily tournaments that started to spring up but nothing with a gigantic payout. As I grew older, wiser, and smarter, I realized that other pros were as good as me and a poker session was like a war. Beating lesser players was easier and more profitable. Beating pros was a chore...when I could do it.

About twelve or fourteen years ago I got even smarter. I decided to stop going into tournaments and taking on these pros because ego does not pay any bills. When there was a tournament in Vegas, I would go out and play against the people who went out with the people who entered the tournaments. They were lesser challengers (fish). Then I would play against the players who got eliminated from the tournaments because obviously they weren't as good as the top pros.

Today I play constantly in New Jersey and never in tournaments. Why play against other pros? To prove what? I already know they're good. There are plenty of lesser players willing to put up their money to see if they can beat me in a regular game. They're not as good as the pros. That's why I'm there!

95

The Author and Discipline

I gamble every day. Seems like I've been gambling since people respected authority and kids knew their parents knew more than them. Now that's really a long time ago! There ain't nothing you can teach me about gambling and yet I win only about 65 percent to 70 percent of the time, regardless of the game.

I like to win and know what it's like to lose. In fact, I used to lose so much there were times I thought it was absolutely impossible to win. It took many years to realize that mostly I lost because I didn't quit when I won a certain amount. I always thought winning was when there were three zeros after the first number. Wrong! Winning is quitting with a profit. Maybe some of you haven't realized that yet.

My biggest fear is that on the day I die, the sports results won't all be in, and I'll head to the game in the sky (or in the furnace) without knowing whether I went out a winner or loser.

Before I was married, there were poker games in the garage, the bowling alley, the Friday night parties, in the back seat of the car on the way home from the shore. (I understand the back seat of the car was also used for other activities... but that's another story. Shows how much gambling overshadowed more important things for me.) Then came the riverboats, the barns in Montana, Wyoming, and Kansas, the sawdust joints, the clubs in New York, and finally, the elaborate casinos.

Sure beats the smoke-filled sixth floor games that went on for four or five days in a shabby hotel where enough money passed across the table to feed China for a year. We had the buzzer backup, where the fifth, sixth, and seventh steps were wired to alert us that unwelcome guests in blue outfits were about to play spoilsports. I always sat near a window which led to a fire escape. While I don't like heights, it sure beat the meals and cots awaiting those who hesitated and tried to explain to the local law that we were really having a prayer meeting.

These games were played against pros who seemed to know the first name of every jack, queen, and king in the deck and when they'd make their appearance. Skill and patience were necessities, talk was minimal, and mercy absent. Make a mistake and the sharks would counter with moves that would make the dead sit up and be amazed. These guys didn't make mistakes and when you thought they did, it'd end up costing you money. You'd leave those games wondering what size tank hit you and from what side. But you learned how to compete. You had better learn or else mail in your donation.

Yeah, I've danced a few dances and had a great run. I've learned things that only come from getting your teeth kicked in and walking the streets wondering where you're gonna get the bread to get back to the tables.

Maybe you realize what I'm trying to say about discipline and maybe some of you will listen. The rest of you? The rest of you will have to get killed to learn your lesson. Rest in Peace!

96

Reality II

The best book I've ever written was *Advanced Craps* with *Sports Handicapping* a close second. That's because they are jammed with money management and discipline theories.

Those of you who read the sports book can skip this chapter because I've reprinted this message in it's entirety from that book.

For those of you who think reality is your wife finally finding out what a dork you are, look at reality as it pertains to gambling. The examples are true and I still have the scars to prove it.

My friend I. M. Smart is the dumbest guy I ever played poker with. But that's why I like him so much. He has lost 862 consecutive poker sessions and calls it a little slump. He also thinks a freezing subzero day is a little chilly, a tornado is a slight breeze, a fall from a roof is a little bumpy, and Dolly Parton looks a tad chunky above the belt.

I didn't say he was smart. He doesn't catch the reality of what is happening around him. As soon as he saw the title of this chapter, a light went on in his brain (it's still totally dark in there) and he screamed, "You already wrote a chapter on reality!"

Yes I did, but I. M. Smart is so stupid I knew he would not grasp it. So I'll pop in another chapter and call it Reality II.

Naturally, you other people are too smart to need another reminder of what I'm gonna say, so why don't you just jump ahead to the next chapter where you believe I'm gonna give you the fact they lost on these games and how could God do this to them. I explained to them that God was probably betting the other side and took matters into his own hands, for his own sake. But mostly I explained to them about those games being the reality of betting sports. Every single statistical edge was in favor of the teams that got beat. Every logical reason to bet on those sides stood out in glaring tones. Would you bet against Maddox or Drabek or the Knicks at home or Michael Jordan plus three points? No way! It wasn't logical.

The reality of sports gambling is that these things happen over and over. If you can't pay the fiddler, don't go on the dance floor.

How did I handle this run of rotten luck? I took the one that caused me the most pain and dealt with it.

I threw the dog out the window!

97

Wrapping Up Poker Knowledge

Usually when I wrap up a section it seems like the proper thing to do is rehash all the main points that were covered. This is not possible in poker or Hold 'Em or Hi/Lo because of all of the intangibles that go into making a good poker player.

The main point is that you gotta get your feet wet to realize what is going on. You gotta ride a bicycle to get the idea. You gotta play in a real game to get the feel. So my suggestion would be to go back and restudy the individual chapters and messages to get the drift and then give yourself a shot at the smaller-limit tables to see if you have what it takes to be a successful poker player.

My friend Iver Gott probably forgot which were the primary points, so I'll list them by poker game, so you can leaf back to those chapters.

SEVEN-CARD STUD:

Pick up tells from other players but don't give any.
Don't talk at a table; avoid giving away hints.
Use fifth street to decide if you'll stay or drop.
If you're dropping too much, throw off opponents with a call when you have two of a suit and both are power cards.
Use fourth street to test the waters with raise if you're strong.

Get out on fifth street if you don't have a quality hand.

Don't raise too much; raise to set up opponent or to get a feel for strong hand against you.

Don't think bluffing is a big part of poker.

Get out when you're beat even if you're strong.

Sixth street is for raising only if you're powerful.

Don't chase straights.

Seldom play on the come.

Don't think you gotta raise the roof on seventh street; a call ain't gonna hurt if you're in doubt.

Realize the other players know the game, too.

HI/LO

Rules are pretty much the same per street as in seven-card stud. A few extra notes:

Key going low.

Zero in on the players who usually go low, and fold when they become aggressive raisers; these rocks only stay when strong.

Send out a raise message to find out where competition is if have three low in four cards.

Learn to read your opponent' hands. (If on fourth street you see player with two high cards on board, you know he is heading high.)

Don't chase. Temptation is strong to chase for low when others appear to be going high. This is dangerous in 8-qualifier games.

HOLD 'EM

Once again the basic moves of going out, raising, and calling at each street are essentially the same. But obviously there are other rules:

Use rankings chart to decide whether to stay or drop when

you get two initial cards.

Remember: Position is all-powerful.

Play cautiously in early position.

Don't be afraid to raise after the flop when in late position and strong.

Call, even in late position, if very powerful (two aces, two kings, ace and king suited) in two cards.

Get out if have not got it in five cards... get it? Because in Hold 'Em, you're gonna see tons of raises on turn card and the river.

Read flops as possible hands against you. You MUST learn possible combinations.

Let it all hang out and make them pay if you're sitting strong and in late position.

These messages are mostly geared to how you handle your cards. But you gotta review the chapters in the areas where you are weakest, and I know you ain't perfect on tells, reading people, or reading the cards on board.

These are the areas where most mistakes happen.

98

Wrapping Up Discipline

All right, I guess you got a bellyful of my harping on money management and discipline, loss limits, win goals, accepting small returns, and all the other messages you think have nothing to do with gambling.

In fact my friend, I. M. Madork, who is the biggest dork at every poker game he plays, asks an obvious question: "I thought poker was all strategy and being better than the other players?"

You'd better be better than the other players. But what about those nights when you're dealt lousy cards and don't have a clue where to cut your losses or when to pack it in? Managing your money and executing strict discipline will allow you to maintain your bankroll for a run on another day.

I. M. Madork nods his head like he knows what I'm saying. But even if he did grasp the message I'm trying to convey, he still wouldn't listen.

And maybe you won't either. If that's the case, you'd better end your poker career and take up something easy—like becoming a window washer on a seventy-eight-story building without a net! That would be easier than trying to win at poker or any form of gambling without discipline.

99

The Ultimate Goal

The answer to playing a conservative, intelligent, rewarding game of poker is covered in this book. Everything is aimed at the ultimate goal, which is to win money. You ain't gonna win every time but you can cut losses and learn to take advantage of good hands when you're at a table that is going good for you.

Hope you learned something from these messages and wish you the very best in your gambling endeavors.

If you need to contact me, my personal address is

GAMBLER
BOX 4333
METUCHEN, NJ 08840
201-992-3862

Happy Winnings
John Patrick

More Books by the World Renowned Gambler and Instructor,
John Patrick

A professional gambler, host of a national television show, as well as creator of dozens of instructional videotapes, John Patrick shares his secrets of success by providing readers with specific, easy-to-learn methods for mastering the tables.

John Patrick's Blackjack
$14.95 paper 0-8184-0555-4 (CAN $19.95)

John Patrick's Advanced Blackjack
$19.95 paper 0-8184-0582-1 (CAN $27.95)

John Patrick's Casino Poker
$17.95 paper 0-8184-0592-9 (CAN $24.95)

John Patrick's Craps
$16.95 paper 0-8184-0554-6 (CAN $23.95)

John Patrick's Advanced Craps
$18.95 paper 0-8184-0577-5 (CAN $26.95)

John Patrick's Roulette
$16.95 paper 0-8184-0587-2 (CAN $23.95)

John Patrick's Slots
$12.95 paper 0-8184-0574-0 (CAN $17.95)

John Patrick's Sports Betting
$17.95 paper 0-8184-0597-X (CAN $24.95)
Available November, 1996

Gambling Books from Carol Publishing Group

Beat the House: Sixteen Ways to Win at Blackjack, Craps, Roulette, Baccarat, and other Table Games by Frederick Lembeck
A unique how-to handbook, applying the system of dollar-cost-averaging used by successful Wall Street investors for years. Much like prices in the stock market, odds in dice, cards, roulette wheels, etc. are always in motion, following a progression of ups and downs—and this is where a mathematical systems profit comes from. Both veteran and novice gamblers can use this book to spell success at every casino table game.
$12.95 paper 0-8065-1607-0 (CAN $17.95)

Beating the Wheel: Winning Strategies at Roulette by Russell T. Barnhart
A system that can be learned quickly and easily for profiting from roulette, based on escalating small bets. In addition to tips on biased-wheel play, wheel-watching systems, electronics, cheating methods and mathematics, readers will also be educated with countless anecdotes from successful players on their own learning experiences.
$14.95 paper 0-8184-0553-8 (CAN $19.95)

Blackjack Your Way to Riches by Richard Albert Canfield
A secret system that shows how it is possible to win at any rate the reader chooses. Includes information on money management and the right method of preserving and building capital, with advice and insight provided by a Las Vegas Strip pit boss and four of the most successful professional Blackjack players in the world today.
$12.95 paper 0-8184-0498-1 (CAN $17.95)

The Cheapskate's Guide to Las Vegas: Hotels, Gambling, Food, Shows, and More by Connie Emerson
How to get maximum satisfaction with minimum expenditure when visiting one of the world's most popular tourist attractions—from pre-trip planning to hotel and restaurant bargains, as well as tips on where to gamble and even which tables to play for the highest payoff with the least amount of capital.
$9.95 paper 0-8065-1530-9 (CAN $13.95)

The Complete Book of Sports Betting: A New, No Nonsense Approach to Sports Gambling by Jack Moore

Introducing the "Blindfold Method," a proven winning system. Moore show how sports bettors can win by putting less emphasis on "handicapping" and focusing on the betting line itself. He provides an informative and entertaining account of the origins of money odds and point spread betting, as well as a clear overview of how, when and why they operate today.

$14.95 paper 0-8184-0579-1 (CAN $20.95)

For Winners Only: The Only Casino Gambling Guide You'll Ever Need by Peter J. Andrews

Andrews offers new insight into the "wrong" betting done by casino gamblers. For example, at the craps table, he abandons traditional rules and recommends betting Don't Pass and Don't Come. With this proven system, based on statistical formulation and analysis—which has won the author in excess of $10 million—gamblers will increase the odds in their favor at all the casino games.

$18.95 paper 0-8065-1728-X (CAN $26.95)

How to Be Treated Like a High Roller...Even Though You're Not One (Revised & Updated) by Robert Renneisen, Introduction by John Patrick

The President of the Claridge Hotel & Casino in Atlantic City reveals how even the most modest gamblers can take advantage of casino giveaways, called "comps," which offer everything from complimentary hotel rooms, dinners, shows, and limousine service to free lunch for each round-trip bus fare.

$8.95 paper 0-8184-0580-5 (CAN $12.95)

Progression Blackjack: Exposing the Card Counting Myth and Getting an Edge in "21" by Donald Dahl

An alternative to card counting—a proven winning strategy for novices and veterans alike which enables you to make more money on winning hands than you lose on losing hands.

$11.95 paper 0-8065-1396-9 (CAN $16.95)

Win at Video Poker: A Guide to Beating the Poker Machines by Roger Fleming

Rules and winning strategies for these gambling machines, including when to redeal, how a big jackpot changes the odds, advice on winning competitions and buy-ins, suggestions on advanced play, and more.

$9.95 paper 0-8065-1605-4 (CAN $13.95)

Prices subject to change; Books subject to availability

the secrets of winning tens of thousands of dollars and show you how to win 80 percent of your games every day.

For those of you who remain, let me say again you're a raving genius if you pick 60 percent winners in sports. The reality of betting on sports and handicapping these games is that you can't properly handicap them. The figures don't hold water, just like the paper those figures are written on can't hold water.

I am writing this chapter on a beautiful spring day in 1996, waiting for the NBA playoffs and baseball games to come on tonight. I am waiting to make my bets on the games that are available. The reason I want the games to begin is to wipe out the stigma of last night's handicapping bonanzas.

I bet the Houston Astros, with former Cy Young Award-winner Doug Drabek pitching, to beat a below .500 St. Louis Cards team. They led 5–1 with Drabek and lost in the ninth inning 6–5. I bet the Atlanta Braves with triple Cy Young pitcher Greg Maddox to beat the below .500 Philadelphia Phils. They led 4–0 with Maddox and lost 5–4 in the ninth inning.

I bet the New York Knicks minus three points to beat the Indiana Pacers. The Knicks led 105–99 with eighteen seconds left. Indiana scored eight points in eleven seconds and lost 107–105. I bet the Chicago Bulls plus three points to beat the Orlando Magic. They led 91–90 with eight seconds to go and Chicago had the ball. Orlando scored four points in six seconds and Michael Jordan had two turnovers in those six seconds. They lost 94–91. (I got a push.)

The phone rang while I was climbing out on the roof to see if I could sprout wings before I hit the ground in a suicide attempt. I came back in and the sexy voice told me she was Dolly Parton wanting to cook dinner for me. As she was giving me her address, my dog bit the phone wire, cutting off Dolly.

And you think you've got problems?

The reality of it is that these things happen and will continue to happen. There were four games that were virtually lock-in winners. Yet each found a way to snatch defeat from the jaws of ecstasy.

I received no less than twenty calls from people lamenting